THE STORY OF
CODEBREAKING

German General Heinz Guderian in his armoured command vehicle during the invasion of France in 1940. To the lower left of the picture is the indispensable Enigma coding machine.

THE STORY OF
CODEBREAKING

From ancient ciphers to quantum cryptography

Al Cimino

ARCTURUS

ARCTURUS

This edition published in 2017 by Arcturus Publishing Limited
26/27 Bickels Yard, 151–153 Bermondsey Street,
London SE1 3HA

ISBN: 978-1-78428-544-9
AD005419UK

Printed in China

Contents

CODEMAKERS VERSUS CODEBREAKERS

'It may be roundly asserted that human ingenuity cannot concoct a cipher which human ingenuity cannot resolve.'

Edgar Allan Poe, 1809–49

Egyptian hieroglyphics seemed to be a code in themselves until cracked using the Rosetta Stone, but sometimes unusual characters were used to render the inscription more arcane.

Throughout history there has always been a need for secrecy. This is because knowledge is power and depriving others of that knowledge gives more power to the powerful. In ancient civilizations, those who possessed the hermetic knowledge of the gods ruled. There are thought to be coded messages in the Torah and in the Bible. Works of the Kabbalah are also encoded.

Works of the Jewish Kabbalah are encoded.

Weapons of war

Codes and ciphers have also been the tools of war – whether overt warfare (for example, safeguarding messages) on the battlefield, or covert warfare fought in the shadows by spies. Joined in battle with those who use encrypted messages to direct troops or steal secrets are the codebreakers. Often, in the face of overwhelming force, they thwart the plans of their enemies using only the power of their intellect.

Julius Caesar used ciphers to communicate with his generals. One of his methods of enciphering remained a key element of ciphers used centuries later. During Europe's Dark Ages, the Arabic world developed new codes and methods of codebreaking, most notably frequency analysis. In Italy during the Renaissance, European codebreaking came into its own again as rival states intrigued and spied on one another.

In England, codebreaking led to the execution of Mary Queen of Scots and played a role in the Gunpowder Plot, while the breaking of a code led to the fall of the Huguenot stronghold of La Rochelle during the religious wars in France. Louis XIV then developed his 'Grand Cipher' as a tool of state. Soon no major European capital was without its 'Black Chamber', where codebreakers operated, intercepting, opening and deciphering coded letters.

Mechanical ciphering

In North America, a mechanical ciphering system was invented by Thomas Jefferson. Other forms were developed during the American Civil War. Also in the 19th century, scientists such as Charles Wheatstone and Charles Babbage, pioneer of the computer, devoted much time and effort to devising and breaking codes. It is thought that Babbage's codebreaking system was

Thomas Phelippes worked for Sir Francis Walsingham's counter-intelligence network, set up to protect the government of Queen Elizabeth I. Phelippes broke the secret code used by Mary Queen of Scots, leading to her execution, and also unmasked the conspirators in the Gunpowder Plot (above).

used during the Crimean War. Meanwhile, codebreaking methods were being used to decipher long-forgotten languages such as Egyptian hieroglyphics and Linear B.

Britain's interception and decoding of the Zimmermann telegram, which revealed Germany's battle plans, brought the USA into World War I. Then, in the 1920s, the US government repudiated the use of codebreaking as ungentlemanly. This left America hopelessly unprepared when war threatened again in the following decade. An intercept that could have warned of the Japanese attack on Pearl Harbor was not decoded in time. Later in World War II, heroic efforts by American cryptologists broke the Japanese naval codes and gave the US Navy the upper hand in the Battle of Midway, which eventually led to victory in the Pacific.

Enigma

Germany had gone into World War II believing it had an unbreakable code – 'Enigma' – not knowing that three inspired Polish codebreakers had already deciphered it before hostilities had even broken out. The Poles passed their expertise and early codebreaking machines on to the British, who used them to good effect throughout the war, and especially in the Battle of Britain and at El Alamein (the latter turned the tide against the German Army in North Africa).

At the British codebreaking centre at Bletchley Park, Alan Turing developed methods and machinery bequeathed by Polish cryptologists to break the more complex Naval Enigma. This thwarted the German U-boats that were threatening to starve Britain into surrender. Later, Bletchley Park's attempt to break the

Posing in front of Colossus, the first large-scale programmable digital computer, are the former Wrens who used to operate it, from left to right: Irene Dixon, Lorna Cockayne, Shirley Wheeldon, Joanna Chorley and Margaret Mortimer. Twelve machines were made in all. They were used at Bletchley Park to break the Lorenz cipher used by the German high command. This reconstructed machine can be seen at the National Museum of Computing at Bletchley.

codes of the German high command's Lorenz cipher was boosted by Post Office engineer Tommy Flowers, who solved the problem by building the first programmable digital computer.

Spies and spying

During the Cold War, codemaking and codebreaking became the stuff of spies. While would-be James Bonds hid messages encrypted on 'one-time pads' under stones in the park, boffins tried to come up with programs which would prevent other boffins from reading the top-secret communications of the government and the military.

In the computer age, codemaking and codebreaking have become the lifeblood of commerce. Vast numbers of financial transactions are performed on the internet, and these must be kept safe from fraudsters and thieves. Huge government organizations, such as American's NSA and Britain's GCHQ, sift through emails, looking for the enciphered communications of terrorists and criminals; while those jealous of our privacy come up with programs to prevent the government snoopers. Even the arcane stuff of quantum physics is now employed by codebreakers and codemakers as the battle between them continues.

During wartime, communication is all important. This collection of World War II vintage equipment – including an Enigma machine at the front – is kept at the National Museum of Military History in Diekirch, Luxembourg.

CHAPTER 1

ANCIENT CIPHERS

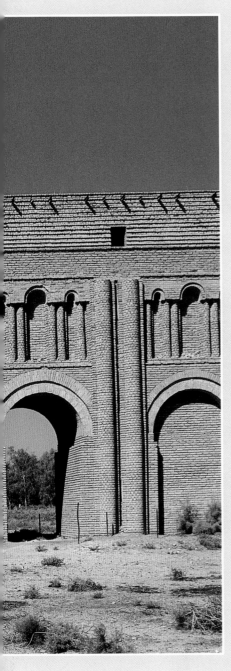

'The art of understanding writing in cypher, and the writing of words in a peculiar way. . . . The art of speaking by changing the forms of words. It is of various kinds. Some speak by changing the beginning and end of words, others by adding unnecessary letters between every syllable of a word, and so on.'

Kama Sutra
3rd century AD

In the ancient world, the art of secret writing was cultivated in the same way that certain professions develop their own jargon and gangs use slang – as a badge of identity and to exclude outsiders. But as warfare grew more sophisticated, code and ciphers became an essential weapon used to communicate strategy and other vital information without tipping your hand to the enemy.

A coded tablet was found at Seleucia, a city in ancient Mesopotamia (now Iraq).

Chinese ideograms make the language unsuitable for ciphers, but the Chinese military made extensive use of codes.

The art of encoding

Inscriptions on the tomb of nobleman Khnumhotep II in the town of Menet Khufu in Egypt substitute unusual symbols for ordinary hieroglyphs. Dating from around 1900BC, this is the oldest known example of a substitution cipher. However, it was not done for the sake of secrecy, but rather to lend kudos to the work and its subject, and to enable the scribe to demonstrate his skill.

As Egyptian civilization progressed, scribes competed with one another to make substitutions like this more complex. Eventually, encoding became so arcane that the inscriptions seemed to be endowed with magical powers. The reader was supposed to be able to figure out the meaning in a reasonably short time, if they were clever enough.

China

In Ancient China, secret messages would be written on very thin silk or paper, then rolled into a ball and covered with wax. This would be hidden about the person, perhaps even inserted in the anus or swallowed. Hiding a message in this way is known as steganography.

The book *Wujing Zongyao*, known in English as the *Complete Essentials for the Military Classics*, outlines a simple code. The first 40 ideograms of a poem correspond to a list of messages ranging from the report of a victory to a request for bows and arrows. The ideogram required would be placed in a specified place in a regular dispatch. The recipient could reply with the same ideogram stamped with their seal, if it was approved, or without their seal, if denied. Even if the dispatch were intercepted, it is unlikely that the enemy would realize the significance of the extra ideogram.

Otherwise the ideographic Chinese alphabet made it unsuitable for ciphers. However, it has been pointed out that, in a country where the literacy rate is low – as it was in the Northern Song Dynasty (970–1127) when *Wujing Zongyao* was written – writing itself is a form of code.

'When these five kinds of spy are all at work, none can discover the secret system. This is called "divine manipulation of the threads". It is the sovereign's most precious faculty.'

Sun Tzu, *The Art of War*

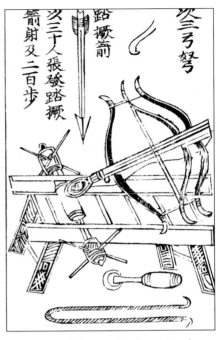

A Chinese triple bow crossbow for use by a four-man team, taken from an illustration in the Wujing Zongyao, *AD1044.*

India

The *Arthashastra*, a treatise on statecraft compiled in the 3rd and 2nd centuries BC, contains a section on spying which extols the use of secret writing. The *Kama Sutra* also mentions that secret writing is one of the 64 arts a woman should know.

While the *Kama Sutra* does not describe the methods used, a commentary on the work written by Yasodhara gives details of two ciphers. One is the Kautilya, named after the author of the *Arthashastra*, in which vowels become consonants according to a chart:

a	ā	i	ī	u	ū	r	ř	ḷ	ḹ	e	ai	o	au	ṃ	ḥ	ñ	ś	ṣ	s	i	r	l	u
kh	g	gh	ṅ	ch	j	jh	ñ	ṭh	ḍ	dh	n	th	d	dh	n	ph	b	bh	n	y	r	l	v

Other letters are left unchanged. There is also a simplified version of the cipher, known as the Durbodha.

The second system was called the Muladeviya, when spoken, and Gudhalekhya, when written. It was used by royal spies and traders, as well as thieves. The following letters are exchanged:

a	kh	gh	c	t	ñ	n	r	l	y
k	g	ṅ	ṭ	p	ṇ	n	ṣ	s	ś

Again the other letters stay the same, though there are regional variations. This secret form of talking appears in the Indian epic narrative *Mahabharata*.

The *Arthashastra* also mentions codebreaking as a way of gathering intelligence. When an agent is unable to determine the loyalty of people directly, it says, 'he may try to gather such information by observing the talk of beggars, intoxicated and insane persons or of persons babbling in sleep, or by observing the signs made in places of pilgrimage and temples or by deciphering paintings and secret writings.'

It does not explain how this is done, but it is the earliest reference to cryptanalysis (the act of deciphering or decoding a message by an unauthorized person) for political purposes.

Mesopotamia

At the site of ancient Seleucia in Iraq, on the banks of the Tigris, a small tablet was found. Dating from about 1500BC and written in cuneiform, it was the formula for making glaze for pottery rendered in a simple code.

It was not unusual for Assyrian and Babylonian scribes to use rare forms of cuneiform letters as a code when signing and dating their clay tablets. This was another way of showing off their knowledge. At Uruk in modern-day Iraq, in the 1st century BC, scribes would encipher the letters of their names as numbers. Comparing tablets using this encryption and others in plaintext (the message before it is encoded), it has been possible to break the code. Fragments of what might be a codebook have been found at Susa, in modern-day Iran. They show columns of numbers opposite cuneiform signs.

Cuneiform tablets from the ancient Middle East sometimes carry codes. This one is in the Museum of Anatolian Civilization in Ankara, Turkey.

The Bible

In the Book of Jeremiah in the Old Testament, a place identifiable as Babel is sometimes called Sheshach; and Leb Kamai, meaning 'heart of my enemy', appears instead of Kashdim, which means the Chaldeans (an indigenous people). These substitutions are made using a system called 'atbash', where the first letter of the alphabet is substituted by the last letter, and vice versa; then the second letter is swapped with the second to last, and so on.

B is the second letter of the Hebrew alphabet, while the second to last is 'sh'. Similarly, the 'l' is replaced with a hard 'ch'. Hebrew is written in consonants only, so Babel becomes *Sheshach*. Meanwhile the hard K of Kashdim becomes an L. Again the 'sh' becomes a 'b', while the final 'i' (or 'yod' in Hebrew) reciprocates with 'mem' in Kamai.

The word 'atbash' reflects the substitution pattern. It is made up of 'aleph', 'taw', 'beth' and 'shin' – the first, last second and next-to-last letters of the Hebrew alphabet. This system of enciphering can be used with any alphabet.

There is thought to be another system of encoding in the Bible called 'albam'. This splits the alphabet into two and substitutes the first letter of the first half for the first letter of the second half, and vice versa. The word itself is made up of the first letter of the first half, followed by the first letter of the second half, the second letter of the first half and the second letter of the second half, and so on.

Secret writing also appears in the Book of Daniel. Like Hebrew, Aramaic is written without vowels. When the words 'MENE

MENE TEKEL PARSIN' appeared on the wall of King Belshazzar's palace, the wise men of Babylon could not read them. So the king sent for Daniel, a Jew. Substituting various vowels, Daniel came up with the interpretation: 'MENE, God has numbered the days of your kingdom and brought it to an end; TEKEL, you have been weighed in the balance and found wanting; PERES, your kingdom is divided and given to the Medes and Persians.' In Aramaic, PERES and PARSIN would have been identical.

Daniel was richly rewarded, but Belshazzar was slain and Darius the Mede took over his kingdom.

Greece

The Ancient Greeks perfected steganography. In Herodotus's *Histories*, which chronicle the conflicts between Greece and Persia in the 5th century BC, he tells of a Greek exile named Demaratus, who witnessed the Persian military build-up and sought to warn Sparta of Xerxes's plans. But how was he to get the message past the Persian guards? Herodotus wrote: 'As the danger of discovery was great, there was only one way in which he could contrive to get the message through: this was by scraping the wax off a pair of wooden folding tablets, writing on the wood underneath

Belshazzar's Feast, *painted in 1635 by Rembrandt van Rijn. The story of Belshazzar and the writing on the wall originates in the Old Testament Book of Daniel. The Babylonian king Nebuchadnezzar looted the Temple in Jerusalem and stole the sacred golden cups. His son Belshazzar used these cups for a great feast where the hand of God appeared and wrote the inscription on the wall prophesying the downfall of his reign.*

what Xerxes intended to do, and then covering the message over with wax again. In this way the tablets, being apparently blank, would cause no trouble with the guards along the road. When the message reached its destination, no one was able to guess the secret, until, as I understand, Cleomenes' daughter Gorgo, who was the wife of Leonidas, divined and told the others that if they scraped the wax off, they would find something written on the wood underneath. This was done; the message was revealed and read, and afterwards passed on to the other Greeks.'

As a result, the Greeks built a navy that defeated the Persians at the Battle of Salamis. Although the Spartans could not hold back the Persian army at Thermopylae, without a fleet to supply his troops Xerxes was forced to withdraw. Leonidas was killed at Thermopylae.

Secret messages helped the Greeks triumph at the Battle of Salamis.

INVISIBLE INK

In the first century AD, the Roman scholar Pliny the Elder described how the sap of the tithymallus plant could be used as invisible milk. When it dried it became transparent, but if heated gently, the milk charred, turning brown. Any organic fluid, rich in carbon, will behave in the same way and spies short of the tools of the trade have been known to use their own urine.

In the 15th century, the Italian scientist Giovanni Porta came up with an even more ingenious solution. He made ink by dissolving alum in vinegar. Then he wrote the message on the shell of a hardboiled egg. The solution passed through the porous shell and stained the hardened egg white beneath. Once the egg was peeled the message could be read.

In another tale, Herodotus tells of a secret message being tattooed on the shaven head of a messenger. Once his hair had grown back, he could safely carry the message to his destination, where his head was shaved again and the message revealed.

Transposition ciphers

One way to encipher a message is to move the letters of the plaintext around in a set fashion. For example, you could reverse every pair of letters so that the message, 'The enemy is going south', ignoring the spaces between words, would become 'Hteeenymsiogngsguoht'. To decrypt, the recipient simply reverses the process.

Another way to do this is to use a 'rail fence' cipher, in which the letters of the plaintext are positioned along parallel lines. The message:

THEENEMYISGOINGSOUTH

is written as:

T E N M I G I G O T
  H E E Y S O N S U H

so the message is rendered:

TENMIGIGOTHEEYSONSUH

You can do this using three or more lines; the message can also be easily deciphered if both sender and recipient use the same number of rails. The message can also be written out in a grid of agreed dimensions.

THEEN
EMYIS

GOING
SOUTH

The encrypted message is then read off vertically as:

TEGSHMOOEYIUEINTNSGH

The Spartans found a way of doing this in the 5th century BC using an implement called a skytale. A narrow strip of leather or parchment was coiled around a baton, then the message was written along the length of the baton, with one letter on each turn of the strip. When the strip was unwound, it carried a long column of jumbled letters. The message could easily be deciphered by winding the strip around a baton of the same dimension as the original.

During the long conflict between Persia and the Greek city states, a captured Spartan messenger who had managed to escape handed Lysander of Sparta his belt. Winding it around his skytale, Lysander discovered that Pharnabazus of Persia, formerly an ally in Sparta's war against Athens, was planning to attack him.

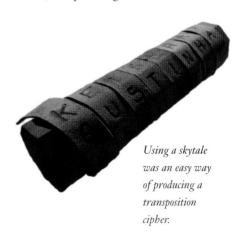

Using a skytale was an easy way of producing a transposition cipher.

Aeneas the Tactician

In the 4th century BC, the Greek writer Aeneas the Tactician devoted a chapter to secret messages in his book *How to Survive Under Siege*. One way he suggests is to use tiny dots to mark letters in a book or document that spell out the message.

A message could be sewn inside the lining of a shoe. It was best to use a thin sheet of tin for this purpose in case the road was wet or muddy. Aeneas reported that a message was brought to Ephesus on leaves bound around a wound on a man's leg. A message could even be sent on thin pieces of lead worn as earrings.

Aeneas also described a method of encoding a message by drilling holes representing the 24 letters of the Greek alphabet in a knucklebone or piece of wood. A thread was then passed through each letter of the message in turn and the message would be revealed by unravelling it.

Polybius square

The Greek historian Polybius, who lived in the 2nd century BC, came up with a system of numerical encryption. He laid the letters of the alphabet in a square 5 x 5. Using the modern English alphabet, the letters I and J appear in a single cell:

	1	2	3	4	5
1	A	B	C	D	E
2	F	G	H	I/J	K
3	L	M	N	O	P
4	Q	R	S	T	U
5	V	W	X	Y	Z

Each letter is represented by two numbers. For example, D = 14; S = 43. To transmit messages over distances, the sender would hold, for example, one torch in his right hand and four torches in his left, giving the number 41 or the letter Q.

Roman ciphers

Julius Caesar used ciphers so frequently that the Roman scholar Valerius Probus wrote a treatise on them. Unfortunately, it has not survived. However, one cipher bearing his name has come down to us. It is the 'Caesar shift cipher'. Caesar simply substituted each letter for another letter three places further down the alphabet, so A became D, B became E . . . and X, Y, Z became A, B, C. Augustus was not quite so adept at enciphering. Suetonius, author of *The Lives of the Twelve Caesars*, wrote: 'When he had occasion to write in cipher, he put b for a, c for b, and so forth; and instead of z, aa.'

Such ciphers were widely used in Roman times. Clearly there was nothing unusual about making a shift of three. In the modern alphabet you could shift anywhere between 1 and 25. Any letter can

> 'A letter containing an offer of betrayal was once conveyed by a traitor into the enemy's camp near at hand in the following manner. One of a troop setting out from the city for a foray had a note sewn up under the skirt of his cuirass, with orders, if the enemy came into view, to fall from his horse as if he had been thrown, and allow himself to be made a prisoner; on arrival in the enemy's camp he was duly to deliver the note.'
>
> Aeneas the Tactician, *How to Survive Under Siege*, 4th century BC

be substituted for any other letter, as long as the recipient knows the key to unscramble it. This means that there are some 403,291,461,126,605,635,584,000,000 possibilities in a simple substitution cipher. It has been estimated that trying to crack a simple alphabetic substitution code by checking each possible permutation every second would take roughly one billion times the age of the universe.

The Gallic chieftain Vercingetorix throws down his arms in surrender to Julius Caesar after the Battle of Alesia. Caesar made extensive use of ciphers. According to the Roman biographer Suetonius: 'If he had anything confidential to say, he wrote it in cipher, that is, by so changing the order of the letters of the alphabet, that not a word could be made out. If anyone wishes to decipher these, and get at their meaning, he must substitute the fourth letter of the alphabet, namely D, for A, and so with the others.'

CLUMSY CODING

Sicilian mafia boss Bernardo Provenzano was captured in 2006 after 40 years on the run because of his clumsy use of the Caesar shift code. Instead of replacing A with D, he replaced A with 4, B with 5 and so on. Ever wary of the danger of using the phone, he ran his crime syndicate using written notes. Once these notes fell into the hands of the police, the code was easy to break.

بسم الله الرحمن الرحيم

... رب العالمين وصلى ... والمرسلين ... محمد خاتم النبيين وعلى ... فإنك ممن يحرص ... عليه وسلم في سنن الدين وأحكامه ... الأخبار المأثورة ... عن رسول ... تعرف جملة ... فإن رحمك الله ... وما كان منها في الثواب ... والترهيب وغير ذلك من صنوف ... فيما بينهم فأردت ... الأشياء بالأسانيد ... وسألتني أن الحظ لك ... ارشدك الله أن توقف ... مما يشغلك عما له قصدت في التأليف بلا تكرار ... موجود ... وظننت حين سألتني ... التفهم فيها والاحتياط ... كان أول من صنف ... وبما يؤول به الحال ... كثيرة يطول ذكرها نفع ذلك أنك ... جامعة ... نفع من العوام المرء أن يحفظ ...

CHAPTER 2

ARABIC ANAGRAMMING

'Occasionally, skilful secretaries, though not the first to invent a code, nonetheless find the rules through combinations which they evolve for the purpose with the help of their intelligence, and which they call "solving the puzzle".'

Ahmad al-Qalqashandi,
Muqqaddimah, 1377

Arab scholars were the first to work out that it was possible to crack a cipher where one letter is substituted for another by calculating the frequency not just of single letters, but pairs of letters and trios that occur in natural language. Reconstructing the plaintext from the clues provided by frequency analysis is called 'anagramming'.

With the flowering of Islamic culture, Arab scholars began writing formal papers on codemaking and codebreaking.

Secret language

While the decline of the Roman Empire and the Dark Ages halted the development of cryptology in the West, the Muslim world was going through a golden age, particularly in mathematics and science. Sensitive state documents, including tax records, were encrypted as a matter of course, and official manuals contained chapters on cryptology.

In the Muslim world's 1st century, the 8th century in the Christian world, the philologist Abu al-Khalil (see box) wrote the *Book of Secret Language*, now sadly lost. It is recorded that al-Khalil first became interested in codes and ciphers when the Byzantine Emperor sent him a cryptogram in Greek, which he could not decipher.

'I said, the letter must begin with "in the name of God" or something of that sort,' said al-Khalil. 'So I worked out its first letters on that basis, and it came right for me.'

A miniature from the Maqamat of al-Hariri showing life under the Abbasid caliphate when Islam spread beyond the Arab world (AD758–1258).

The lexicographer and philologist Abu al-Khalil.

ABU AL-KHALIL (718–786)

Abu al-Khalil (or al-Farahidi) was born in Oman. When he moved to Basra, where he taught and was at one time secretary to the vizier, he converted from the Ibadi sect of Islam to Sunnism. He lived piously in a small house made of reeds and wrote *Kitab al-'Ayn* ('Book of the Letter') which is regarded as the first Arabic dictionary. Verses from his *Kitab al-'Arud* ('Book of Prosody') survive though, like his *Book of Secret Language*, the book itself is lost. He was also well versed in astronomy, mathematics, Islamic law, music theory and Muslim prophetic tradition, and influenced the Arab cryptographers who came after him. It is said that he died when he absent-mindedly bumped into a pillar in a mosque while figuring out in his head an accounting system that would prevent his housemaid being cheated by the greengrocer. The resulting fall killed him.

Frequency analysis

In the 9th century, the polymath Abu al-Kindî (see box) – 'the philosopher of the Arabs' – was working out of a major intellectual centre, known as the House of Wisdom, in Baghdad. In a manuscript entitled *On Deciphering Encrypted Correspondence* he outlined how to decode a document by frequency analysis, the study of the number of times certain letters or letter groups appear in coded text. He wrote:

> 'One way to solve an encrypted message, if we know its language, is to find a different plaintext of the same language long enough to fill one sheet or so, and then we count the occurrences of each letter. We call the most frequently occurring letter the "first", the next most occurring letter the "second", the following most occurring the "third", and so on, until we account for all the different letters in the plaintext sample.

> 'Then we look at the cipher text we want to solve and we also classify its symbols. We find the most occurring symbol and change it to the form of the "first" letter of the plaintext sample, the next most common symbol is changed to the form of the "second" letter, and so on, until we account for all symbols of the cryptogram we want to solve.'

This was the beginning of systematic cryptanalysis. Al-Kindî noted that, in Arabic, the letters *alif* and *lām* appear most frequently, as they are part of the definite article 'al-', while the letter 'j' appears only a tenth as often.

In this 13th-century miniature entitled The best rulings and the most precious sayings of Al-Mubashshir, *the figure on the right is thought to be Abu al Kindî.*

ABU AL-KINDî (c.801–873)

Abu al-Kindî was hailed as the father of Islamic or Arab philosophers for his promotion of Greek and Hellenistic philosophy in the Muslim world. Born in Basra, he was educated in Baghdad where the caliphs appointed him to oversee the translation of Greek scientific and philosophical works into Arabic. He also wrote on diverse subjects including metaphysics, ethics, logic, psychology, medicine, pharmacology, mathematics, astronomy, astrology, optics, perfumes, swords, jewels, glass, dyes, zoology, tides, mirrors, meteorology and earthquakes. He played a key part in the introduction of Indian numerals, which for the first time employed a symbol for zero. Our modern numerical system is all thanks to al-Kindî. It is thought that a lot of his work was lost when the Mongols destroyed the libraries during an invasion in the 13th century.

The frequency of letters in English

In English, 'e' is the most frequently used letter, followed by 't', then 'a'. So if the letter 'p' is the most frequently found letter in a piece of cipher text, then 'p' most likely represents 'e' in the plaintext. And if the second most frequently found letter in the cipher text is 'x', then this most likely stands for 't' in the plaintext.

The results, shown in the box (below), were based on more than 100,000 characters of text taken from newspapers and novels.

LETTER	PERCENTAGE OF TIMES USED
A	8.167
B	1.492
C	2.782
D	4.253
E	12.702
F	2.228
G	2.015
H	6.094
I	6.966
J	0.153
K	0.772
L	4.025
M	2.406
N	6.749
O	7.507
P	1.929
Q	0.095
R	5.987
S	6.327
T	9.056
U	2.758
V	0.978
W	2.360
X	0.150
Y	1.974
Z	0.074

Source: *Cipher Systems: The Protection of Communication* by H. Beker and F. Piper

Of course, the percentages will vary in specialized text, such as technical and scientific works.

It should be possible to pick out the three most frequent letters, representing 'e', 't' and 'a', in a relatively short piece of cipher text. Then the cryptanalyst needs to look at the letters next to them. Vowels tend to appear before and after consonants more often than other consonants. If you combine this knowledge with the frequency of the most common letters, it soon becomes clear which is 't' and which are 'e' and 'a'.

There are other clues. In English, the digraph 'ee' is quite common, while 'aa' is exceedingly rare. Similarly, 'ea' is much more common than 'ae'.

Another frequently used letter is 'h'. It is easy to spot because it often occurs before (but seldom after) 'e', and often after (but rarely before) 't'.

The Muqaddimah and Dawn for the Blind

In 1377, the North African historian Ibn Khaldûn (see box) completed the *Muqaddimah* ('The Introduction'), which says: 'Occasionally, skilful secretaries, though not the first to invent a code, nonetheless find the rules through combinations which they evolve for the purpose with the help of their intelligence, and which they call "solving the puzzle".' In other words, they could decipher a code of which they had no previous knowledge.

The Egyptian writer and mathematician Ahmad al-Qalqashandi (see box on page 29) completed the 14-volume encyclopaedia *Subh al-a'sha* (*The Dawn for the Blind*) in 1412. He included a section on cryptology,

It was not uncommon for the makers of tombstones, such as those found at the ancient port of Al-Baleed in Oman, to include occult language which would only have meaning to those who knew the deceased.

IBN KHALDÛN (1332–1406)

Walî al-Dîn Ibn Khaldûn was born in Tunis to a family of refugees who had fled the fall of Seville during the Christian reconquest of Spain. At 17 he was orphaned by the Black Death. At 20, he put his classical Islamic education to use at the court of Tunis, moving on to become secretary to the sultan of Morocco three years later. After being imprisoned for suspected sedition, he was sent to Granada, successfully concluding a peace treaty with Pedro I of Castile, also known as 'Pedro the Cruel'. A victim of political intrigues, Ibn Khaldûn moved back to North Africa where he became prime minister under the sultan of Bougie. He served in political office under various potentates, before being jailed again. Seeking sanctuary with the Berbers, he spent his time working on a planned history of the world, of which the *Muqaddimah* is the introduction. To complete his work, he needed access to a

The History of Beni Abd El-Wad – *it was in there that, once again, Ibn Khaldûn's political manoeuvrings got him into trouble.*

library, so he returned to Tunis, which had been conquered by his former employer the sultan of Tlemcen. Falling into disfavour, Ibn Khaldûn asked permission to make the Hajj to Mecca, a request the sultan could not refuse. Instead, Ibn Khaldûn sailed for Alexandria. In Egypt, he dabbled in politics again, spending his last years in Cairo where he completed his history of the world and his autobiography, before dying at the age of 74.

attributing its contents to Ibn al-Durayhim, who lived from 1312 to 1361, but whose writings on ciphers had been lost for centuries.

According to Qalqashandi, Durayhim outlined seven types of cipher:

1. Replacing one letter with another.
2. Writing the word backwards.
3. Reversing alternate letters.
4. Using numerical values of the letter and writing the message in Arabic numerals.
5. Multiple substitutions, such as using two letters for each plaintext letter.
6. Substituting the name of a man (or similar) for each letter.
7. Substituting the lunar houses for letters; or using the names of countries, trees, fruits and so on, in a certain order; or replacing letters with drawings of birds or other creatures, listed in a certain order; or simply inventing a new system of symbols.

Teaching how to decipher

Qalqashandi maintained that the cryptanalyst must know the language in which the cryptogram is written. Concentrating on Arabic, he listed letters which seldom appear together in a word. He gave the letter frequency found in the Koran, noting that it might be different in other texts. He then set out how to go about deciphering a cryptogram, again citing Durayhim:

'When you want to solve a message which you have received in code, begin first of all by counting the letters, and then count how many times each symbol is reported and set down the totals individually. If the person devising the code has been very thorough and has concealed the word-divisions in the body of the message, then the first thing to be worked out is the symbol which divides up the words. To do this, you take a letter and work on the assumption that the next letter is the word-divider. Then you go all through the message with it, having regard for

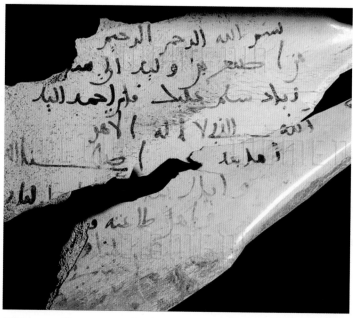

With paper still a rare commodity, here code is written on a camel's shoulder bone.

the possible combinations of letters which the word may be composed of, as has been explained previously. If it fits, [ok]; if not, take the next letter. If that fits, [ok]; if not, take the next letter, and so on, until you ascertain the division of the words.

'Next, look at which letters occur most frequently in the message, and compare this with the pattern of letter-frequency mentioned before. When you see that one letter occurs in the message more often than the rest, then assume that it is alif*; then assume that the next most frequent is* lâm*. The accuracy of your conjecture should be confirmed by the fact that mostly* lâm *follows* alif*. . . .*

'Then the first words which you try to work out in the message are the two-lettered ones, though estimating the most feasible combinations of their letters, until you are sure you have discovered something correct in them; then look at their symbols and write down the equivalents. Apply the same principle to the message's three lettered-words until you are sure you have got something, then write out the same equivalents [throughout the message]. Apply the same principle to the previous procedure.'

Qalqashandi then gave practical examples, demonstrating how this was done. But his methods did not spread quickly in the Muslim world. In 1600, the Sultan of Morocco, Ahmed al-Mansur, sent his confidential secretary to Elizabeth I of England to negotiate an alliance against Spain. The ambassador sent back a coded

A portrait of Abd el-Ouahed ben Messaoud, the ambassador sent to negotiate with Elizabeth I.

message, which took the recipients 15 years to decipher! Had they followed the method laid out by Durayhim, the process would have taken just a few hours.

Anagramming

If the cryptographer leaves in the spaces between words, the text will contain relatively easy clues. For example, in English there are only two one-letter words – 'a' and 'I'. And there are relatively few common two-letter words – 'ah', 'am', 'an', 'as', 'at', 'be', 'do', 'go', 'ha', 'he', 'hi', 'if', 'id', 'in', 'is', 'it', 'me', 'my', 'no', 'of', 'oh', 'ok', 'on', 'ox', 'so', 'to', 'up', 'us', 'we', 'ye'… so finding one-letter and two-letter words gives the codebreaker a head start.

Tables of the most frequent bigrams and trigrams (groups of two or three characters that may be coded as a unit) have been made.

Using frequency analysis of letters, bigrams and trigrams, it is possible to work out the substitution for a good proportion of a cipher. Reconstructing the plaintext in this fashion is called 'anagramming', though it has little to do with anagrams in the conventional sense. Sometimes there may be a weakness in the encipherment that makes the job of decoding the cryptogram a whole lot easier.

The Book of Songs is an anthology of early Arabic poetry that not only has literary value, but is also important from a cultural and historical perspective. The ruler is wearing a 'qaba turki' robe. On his head is a 'sharbush'. His attendants also wear Turkish costumes. The ruler is generally identified with Badr al-Din Lulu, Atabeg of Mosul, who died in AD1259. It illustrates the wealth of knowledge in early Arabic history.

AHMAD AL-QALQASHANDI (1355/6–1418)

Born in a village in the Nile Delta, writer and mathematician Ahmad al-Qalqashandi was working for the Mamluk sultanate in Cairo when he wrote the 14-volume encyclopaedia *Subh al-a'sha* (*The Dawn for the Blind*), which covered geography, political history, natural history, zoology, mineralogy, cosmography, the measurement of time and cryptography. Quoting Ibn al-Durayhim, Qalqashandi lists ciphers which use both substitution and transposition and, for the first time, a cipher that uses multiple substitutions for each plaintext letter. He also includes tables of letter frequencies and sets of letters that cannot occur together in one word.

To encrypt messages, it is best not to depend on a codebook, which can be captured by the enemy. It's better to commit a method of encipherment to memory. One way is to use a key – the word ENGLAND, say. First, strip out any repetitions of letters in the key, to give (in this case) ENGLAD. Lodge this at the beginning of the cipher alphabet, running the rest of the alphabet after it, again avoiding repetitions.

Plain alphabet

a b c d e f g h i j k l m n o p q r s t u v w x y z

Cipher alphabet

ENGLADBCFHIJKMOPQRSTUVWXYZ

The key does not necessarily have to fall at the beginning of the cipher alphabet.

BIGRAMS AND TRIGRAMS

Drawn from 10,000 letters taken from military orders or reports, the *Manual for the Solution of Military Ciphers* by Parker Hitt (see page 79), published in 1915, gives the following:

MOST FREQUENT BIGRAMS		MOST FREQUENT TRIGRAMS	
TH	50	THE	89
ER	40	AND	54
ON	39	THA	47
AN	38	ENT	39
RE	36	ION	36
HE	33	TIO	33
IN	31	FOR	33
ND	30	NDE	31
ED	30	HAS	28
HA	26	NCE	27
AT	25	EDT	27
EN	25	TIS	25

> 'Whenever there is any doubt, postulate two or three or more conjectures and write each down until it becomes certain from another word.'
>
> Ahmad al-Qalqashandi, 1412

Plain alphabet

a b c d e f g h i j k l m n o p q r s t u v w x y z

Cipher alphabet

WXYZENGLADBCFHIJKMOPQRSTUV

The key works provided that both sender and recipient put it in the same place. If the key is a single word, it is relatively easy for the cryptanalyst to spot and break the code. But it could be a phrase or a line of poetry, which would be harder to decipher. Of course, if the key is 26 letters long, it will scramble the cipher alphabet completely.

TAX CODES

In the Arabic world, a special form of cryptography called 'qirmeh' was used by tax officials to keep sensitive information concerning state revenues secret. Arabic letters were simplified and accents and other diacritic points were abandoned. The body of the letter was reduced in size, while the tail was elongated. Words were then abbreviated, run together, intermingled and superimposed. This system was first used in Egypt in the 16th century and was taken up by the tax authorities of the Ottoman Empire. It continued in use in Egypt, Syria and Istanbul until the late 19th century when the Ottoman Empire was in decline. Although it was successful in keeping the details of the state finances secret, and maintained the privacy of taxpayers, qirmeh was only ever used in documents on tax affairs. No attempts were made to put it to military use; nor was it used in espionage.

The Baghdad House of Wisdom was a major intellectual centre during the Islamic Golden Age.

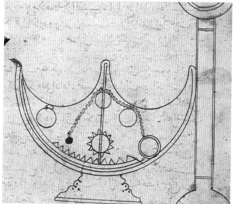

The House of Wisdom would have been illuminated by self-trimming lamps, such as the one shown here in a book on mechanical devices.

IBN AL-DURAYHIM (1312–61)

Born in Mosul, Alî ibn Muhammad Ibn al-Durayhim was a child when his father died, leaving him heir to a huge fortune. Once he was old enough, he travelled to Damascus, then on to Cairo, where he invested his money in trade. He also worked for the Mamluk sultans there. In 1347, he was exiled from Cairo and separated from much of his money. The following year, he was exiled from Damascus to Aleppo. Eventually collecting some of his money from Cairo, al-Durayhim became a teacher at the Amawî Mosque in Damascus and worked in the finance department there. After returning to Egypt, he became involved in politics and was exiled again, this time to Abyssinia. On his way there, he died at the town of Qus, an important commercial centre just north of Luxor. During his short life, he compiled more than 20 books on Muhammad, the Koran, science, the Arabic language, physiognomy, riddles and puzzles, and wrote well-regarded poetry. His statistical method of codebreaking using letter frequency was taken up by al-Kindi and others.

Though opulent, the court of the Mamluk sultans was full of deadly political rivalries.

CHAPTER 3

EUROPEAN ENCIPHERERS

'No enterprise is more likely to succeed than one concealed from the enemy until it is ripe for execution.'

Niccolo Machiavelli,
1469–1527

From the 16th century onwards, warring states resorted to codes and ciphers to out-manoeuvre their enemies. Professional codebreakers were employed by Venice and the Vatican. Cryptology became an arm of the state. Ever more sophisticated codes were devised and soon every nation boasted its own 'Black Chamber' of cryptanalysts keeping an eye on the secret activities of its rivals.

The European courts were full of secrecy and intrigue, often conducted with coded notes.

Early spies

While Arabic scholars were making great strides in cryptanalysis, Europeans were still using simple monoalphabetic substitution ciphers (where one letter is always substituted for another in the plaintext). Then, in the 16th century, along came Europe's first great codebreaker, Giovanni Soro, cipher secretary to the Council of Ten which governed Venice. Soro's success at codebreaking for the Council was so great that his reputation spread throughout Italy. As a result, the pope hired him to break codes that his own cipher analysts in Rome could not crack. Once, when a coded papal message fell into the hands of the Florentines, Pope Clement VII sent a copy to Soro, who reported that he could not break it. This may have been a bit of crafty politicking, as Soro would hardly have wanted the Vatican to come up with codes more secure than his own.

The French were hard at work too. Philibert Babou (1484–1557), codebreaker to Francis I, worked long hours cracking ciphers while the king took his pretty wife as his mistress.

The Council of Ten ruled Venice. It consisted of the Doge and nine councillors and employed the great Giovanni Soro as cipher secretary.

GIOVANNI SORO (d.1544)

In the warring Italian city states, ambassadors communicated via coded messages. Consequently, governments employed cipher clerks to decrypt intercepted missives. The Council of Ten in Venice employed Giovanni Soro to this post in 1506. When the Republic of Venice was menaced by the army of the Holy Roman Emperor Maximilian I, Soro broke the code of a dispatch from the army's commander Mark Anthony Colonna, asking for 20,000 ducats or the presence of Maximilian on the battlefield. This showed that the commander was too weak to put up much of a fight. Maximilian's alliance with the pope split apart and, in 1510, the papal curia began using Soro as a codebreaker. Nevertheless, Soro's first loyalty remained to Venice. In 1542, he was given two assistants and an office in the Doge's Palace. They worked behind locked doors and were not allowed to leave before a message had been decoded. Venice had a school for ciphering and held contests. Soro wrote a manual on the subject which was, sadly, lost.

Cipher text and plaintext decrypted by Soro.

The Babington Plot

In England, codebreaking brought about the downfall of Mary Queen of Scots. Having fled her homeland in 1568, Mary sought sanctuary in England but was imprisoned by her Protestant cousin, Queen Elizabeth I, because of the perceived threat she posed. Many English Catholics considered Mary the rightful queen. In 1586, Catholic nobleman Anthony Babington hatched a plot to free Mary and assassinate Elizabeth. Letters were smuggled to Mary in the hollow bung of a beer barrel. They were in code, which consisted of 23 symbols representing the letters of the alphabet, excluding 'j', 'v' and 'w'. Another 36 symbols represented common words or phrases. To muddy the waters further, there were four nulls, symbols that represent nothing, added simply to confuse anyone who intercepted the message and tried to decipher it. There was another symbol which signified that the next symbol in the message represented a double letter.

Gilbert Gifford, the conspirator who had been entrusted with delivering the letters, was a double agent. He handed them to Sir Francis Walsingham, Queen Elizabeth's principal secretary and spymaster who had them copied. Walsingham was familiar with the work of the Italian mathematician and cryptographer Girolamo Cardano and had benefited from the work of Flemish cryptanalyst Philip van Marnix, who was cipher clerk to William of Orange. In 1577, Marnix had deciphered a letter from Philip of Spain, outlining his plans to invade England. This was handed to the English, who reinforced their defences sufficiently to deter the Spanish invasion attempt, or at least delay it until the Armada set sail 11 years later.

Walsingham's 'Decypherer' Thomas Phelippes forged this cipher postscript to Mary Queen of Scots' letter to Babington. It asks Babington to use the (broken) cipher to tell her the names of the conspirators.

Walsingham set up a spy school and employed linguist Thomas Phelippes (see box opposite) as a codebreaker. Using frequency analysis, Phelippes set about breaking Babington's code. He soon identified the nulls and, after cracking the letter substitutions, guessed the code words from their context. Babington and six co-conspirators were arrested and hanged. Then, according to chronicler William Camden, 'they were cut down, their privities were cut off, bowelled alive and seeing, and quartered.'

Tried for treason at Fotheringhay Castle, Mary denied all knowledge of the plot. The deciphered correspondence proved otherwise. She was beheaded on 8 February 1587.

The Alberti cipher disc

The Babington plot demonstrated that more sophisticated ciphers were needed.

> 'There is nothing more dangerous than security.'
>
> Francis Walsingham, 1532–90

The conspirators of the Gunpowder Plot underwent a gruesome death, but although Phelippes was implicated by Guy Fawkes he escaped with a mere four years' imprisonment in the Tower of London.

THOMAS PHELIPPES (1556–1625)

Educated at Cambridge, Thomas Phelippes could speak French, Italian, Latin, German and Spanish. However, his appearance was unprepossessing. He was described by Mary Queen of Scots as a man 'of low stature, slender every way, dark yellow haired on the head, and clear yellow beard, eaten in the face with smallpox, of short sight, 30 years of age by appearance.' When Francis Walsingham became principal secretary to Elizabeth I in 1573, he recruited Phelippes to his spy school. Phelippes' duties were 'cryptographer, forger and gatherer of secret correspondence'. Not only did he break the code Babington and Mary Queen of Scots were using, he also forged a postscript to one of Mary's letters requesting the names of Babington's co-conspirators. He continued working as the linchpin in Walsingham's extensive intelligence service, exchanging encoded messages with agents in Scotland, France and the Netherlands, collecting codes and ciphers, and deciphering intercepted letters. When Walsingham died, the intelligence service was taken over by the queen's favourite, Robert Devereux, Earl of Essex, who employed Phelippes to investigate another supposed plot. Although the alleged conspirators were executed, the queen was not convinced of their guilt and Phelippes fell out of favour. Heavily in debt, he was incarcerated in the Marshalsea, an infamous South London prison. When James I came to the throne, Phelippes returned to the intelligence service and was involved in apprehending the conspirators in the Gunpowder Plot. However, Guy Fawkes claimed that close friends of Phelippes were involved in the plot and Phelippes was imprisoned in the Tower of London for over four years. After another spell in the debtors' prison, he died around 1625.

Their development had begun the previous century when, in 1467, Italian architect and polymath Leon Battista Alberti wrote a treatise on cryptanalysis that contained the first known frequency table. This showed the inherent weakness of monoalphabetic substitution, where a message is enciphered using just one substitution alphabet. Alberti realized that, if you used more than one substitution alphabet and switched between them, this would confuse any codebreaker. To that end, he described what has become known as an Alberti cipher disc.

It consisted of two flat copper circles with a common axis so that they could rotate relative to each other. The edge of each circle was divided into 24 cells. On the outer circle, Alberti put the letters in the alphabet, in capitals, in each cell, omitting 'H', 'K' and 'Y'. As the Latin and Italian alphabets have no 'J', 'U' and 'W', this gave him four empty cells which he filled with the numbers 1 to 4. On the inner circle, he put the letters of the alphabet in lower case in a random order. The disk came with a

As well as designing the church of St Andrew in Mantua, Alberti wrote a treatise on cryptanalysis including the first known frequency table.

codebook of 336 phrases with numerical values, generated by the numbers 1 to 4, which were also encoded as lower-case letters by the disc.

A starting position is fixed on the inner ring. Its corresponding letter on the outer ring is given as a capital letter. The message is then encoded by reading across from the upper-case letters to the lower-case letters beneath them. Every so often, a new capital letter is inserted in the message. The starting point on the lower circle is then moved under that letter and the encoding starts again, essentially using a different cipher alphabet.

There are other methods for the encoder to signal to the decoder, who has an identical disc, when to alter their relative positions. The sender could simply encipher one of the numbers. The lower-case letter then given is moved under the A. It doesn't matter how this shift is done as long as both sender and recipient are using the same method, and the shift is made several times during the encryption.

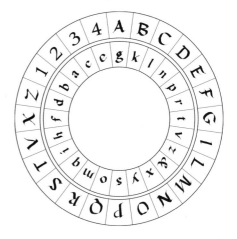

The Alberti cipher disc.

Le chiffre indéchiffrable

The idea of polyalphabetic substitution developed slowly. Eventually, in a system attributed to French diplomat Blaise de Vigenère (see box below), 26 cipher alphabets were used. This became known as *le chiffre indéchiffrable*, or 'the unbreakable cipher'.

THE VIGENÈRE SQUARE

The code is laid out in what is known as a Vigenère square. Along the top are the letters of the alphabet. Under this, the alphabet is repeated but given a Caesar shift of one. The next line has a Caesar shift of two, and so on, until there are 26 lines.

	a	b	c	d	e	f	g	h	i	j	k	l	m	n	o	p	q	r	s	t	u	v	w	x	y	z
1	B	C	D	E	F	G	H	I	J	K	L	M	N	O	P	Q	R	S	T	U	V	W	X	Y	Z	A
2	C	D	E	F	G	H	I	J	K	L	M	N	O	P	Q	R	S	T	U	V	W	X	Y	Z	A	B
3	D	E	F	G	H	I	J	K	L	M	N	O	P	Q	R	S	T	U	V	W	X	Y	Z	A	B	C
4	E	F	G	H	I	J	K	L	M	N	O	P	Q	R	S	T	U	V	W	X	Y	Z	A	B	C	D
5	F	G	H	I	J	K	L	M	N	O	P	Q	R	S	T	U	V	W	X	Y	Z	A	B	C	D	E
6	G	H	I	J	K	L	M	N	O	P	Q	R	S	T	U	V	W	X	Y	Z	A	B	C	D	E	F
7	H	I	J	K	L	M	N	O	P	Q	R	S	T	U	V	W	X	Y	Z	A	B	C	D	E	F	G
8	I	J	K	L	M	N	O	P	Q	R	S	T	U	V	W	X	Y	Z	A	B	C	D	E	F	G	H
9	J	K	L	M	N	O	P	Q	R	S	T	U	V	W	X	Y	Z	A	B	C	D	E	F	G	H	I
10	K	L	M	N	O	P	Q	R	S	T	U	V	W	X	Y	Z	A	B	C	D	E	F	G	H	I	J
11	L	M	N	O	P	Q	R	S	T	U	V	W	X	Y	Z	A	B	C	D	E	F	G	H	I	J	K
12	M	N	O	P	Q	R	S	T	U	V	W	X	Y	Z	A	B	C	D	E	F	G	H	I	J	K	L
13	N	O	P	Q	R	S	T	U	V	W	X	Y	Z	A	B	C	D	E	F	G	H	I	J	K	L	M
14	O	P	Q	R	S	T	U	V	W	X	Y	Z	A	B	C	D	E	F	G	H	I	J	K	L	M	N
15	P	Q	R	S	T	U	V	W	X	Y	Z	A	B	C	D	E	F	G	H	I	J	K	L	M	N	O
16	Q	R	S	T	U	V	W	X	Y	Z	A	B	C	D	E	F	G	H	I	J	K	L	M	N	O	P
17	R	S	T	U	V	W	X	Y	Z	A	B	C	D	E	F	G	H	I	J	K	L	M	N	O	P	Q
18	S	T	U	V	W	X	Y	Z	A	B	C	D	E	F	G	H	I	J	K	L	M	N	O	P	Q	R
19	T	U	V	W	X	Y	Z	A	B	C	D	E	F	G	H	I	J	K	L	M	N	O	P	Q	R	S
20	U	V	W	X	Y	Z	A	B	C	D	E	F	G	H	I	J	K	L	M	N	O	P	Q	R	S	T
21	V	W	X	Y	Z	A	B	C	D	E	F	G	H	I	J	K	L	M	N	O	P	Q	R	S	T	U
22	W	X	Y	Z	A	B	C	D	E	F	G	H	I	J	K	L	M	N	O	P	Q	R	S	T	U	V
23	X	Y	Z	A	B	C	D	E	F	G	H	I	J	K	L	M	N	O	P	Q	R	S	T	U	V	W
24	Y	Z	A	B	C	D	E	F	G	H	I	J	K	L	M	N	O	P	Q	R	S	T	U	V	W	X
25	Z	A	B	C	D	E	F	G	H	I	J	K	L	M	N	O	P	Q	R	S	T	U	V	W	X	Y
26	A	B	C	D	E	F	G	H	I	J	K	L	M	N	O	P	Q	R	S	T	U	V	W	X	Y	Z

To encode a message using the Vigenère square, you need a key word – BLUE, say. Then you use the lines of the Vigenère square starting with each letter in turn.

Message	s e n d c a n n o n t o t h e h i l l t o p
Key	BLUEBLUEBLUEBLUEBLUEBL
Ciphertext	TPHHDLHRPYNSUSYLJWFXPZ

> 'He had just told me that a great number of letters in cipher of the king of Spain as of the [Holy Roman] Emperor and of other princes that had been intercepted, which he had deciphered and interpreted.'
> Giovanni Mocenigo, Venetian ambassador to France, 15 March 1589

To decode the message, the recipient needs the key word, then he or she simply reverses the process.

The strength of the Vigenère cipher is that it cannot be cracked using frequency analysis. The most common letter in the example above is 'H', but it doesn't correspond to the most common letter in the English language, which is 'e'. Here it represents 'd' and on two occasions 'n'. And the three 'n's in 'cannon' are represented by 'H', 'R' and 'Y'. The codebreaker has a further problem in that the key can be any word or phrase, or even a random selection of letters. It can be changed at any time, provided both sender and recipient are in agreement.

Homophonic substitution

Despite its obvious merits, the Vigenère cipher was slow to catch on because using it took time and effort and, in battle, speed is of the essence. Monoalphabetic substitution ciphers were still used, even though they could be broken. The hope was that by the time the cipher had been cracked, the appropriate military action would have been taken and the content of the message would be out of date and, therefore, useless.

For more secure correspondence, a homophonic substitution cipher was used. This is where letters of the plaintext are replaced by two or more letters, figures or graphic symbols. More substitutes are given to the letters that occur most frequently. As 'e' accounts for roughly 13 per cent of all letters written in English, if there were 13 symbols that could be substituted for it and they were picked at random, then each symbol would only appear 1 per cent

---

BLAISE DE VIGENÈRE (1523–96)

Born to a noble family, Blaise de Vigenère was given a classical education in Paris, studying both Greek and Hebrew. He entered the diplomatic service and, in 1549, went to Rome on a two-year diplomatic mission (he returned in 1566). In Rome he had contact with cryptologists and read books about cryptography published there. He published his own *Traicté des Chiffres ou Secrètes Manières d'Escrire* (*Treatise on Ciphers or Secret Ways of Writing*) in 1586, the very year that Thomas Phelippes was deciphering the correspondence between Babington and Mary Queen of Scots. Had the Catholic conspirators used Vigenère's system, it's unlikely they would have been discovered.

The frontispiece of an art book by Vigenère, published in Paris in 1615.

The Grand Cipher of Louis XIV

Codebreaker Antoine Rossignol came to prominence when the Catholic armies under Cardinal Richelieu were besieging the Huguenot stronghold of La Rochelle. Rossignol deciphered a coded letter which revealed that the city's starving citizens were expecting to be relieved by an English fleet. The letter and Rossignol's deciphered version were returned to the Huguenots

Antoine Rossignol.

of the time in the ciphertext. Similarly, as 'a' appears roughly 8 per cent of the time, eight symbols would be substituted at random, defying frequency analysis.

Nevertheless, there were still clues that the dedicated cryptanalyst could use to break the cipher. For example, 'q' accounts for less than 0.1 per cent of letters appearing in the English language, so it is likely to be represented by only one symbol. In English, 'q' is invariably followed by 'u', which occurs roughly 3 per cent of the time, so is likely to be represented by three symbols.

and they were forced to surrender under the eyes of the English, who were held at bay.

Rossignol moved on to work for Louis XIII whose successor, Louis XIV, also recognized Rossignol's worth and employed him at Versailles, giving the codebreaker a room next to the king's study. A courtier described Rossignol as 'the most skilful decipherer of Europe.... No cipher escaped him; there were many which he read right

The king's study at Versailles – Rossignol's cipher room was next door.

away. This gave him many intimacies with the king, and made him an important man.'

With his son, Bonaventure, Rossignol developed the Grand Cipher. This combined nomenclators (lists of names which can be substituted one for another) or code words with homophonic substitutions. There were also nulls and code groups which were merely an instruction to ignore the previous code group. After the death of Bonaventure's son, the Grand Cipher fell into disuse. Soon, enciphered records in the French archives could no longer be read. It was only in 1890 that the Grand Cipher was broken. A historian requested that Commandant Étienne Bazeries, a codebreaker with the French Army's Cryptographic Department, go to work on some of Louis XIV's encrypted orders. It took Bazeries three years to crack the cipher.

One of the letters that Bazeries deciphered referred to the Man in the Iron Mask, a mysterious prisoner first incarcerated in the French fort at Pignerol,

Savoy (now Pinerolo in Piedmont) in 1681, who died in the Bastille in 1703. The message identifies him as the disgraced General Vivien de Bulonde (though other theories persist).

Black Chambers

Following the Rossignols, codebreakers reading the ciphered dispatches of foreign diplomats were consigned to the Cabinet Noir, or Black Chamber. Throughout the 18th century, Black Chambers were set up in various European capitals. The most famous was the Geheime Kabinets-Kanzlei in Vienna. Letters going to the various embassies would arrive at the Black Chamber at 7 a.m.; they were opened and copied, then resealed and returned to the post office for delivery. Dispatches simply passing through Austria arrived at 10 a.m.; letters sent out by the embassies arrived at 4 p.m. Around 100 letters a day were copied and handed over to the codebreakers.

The Geheime Kabinets-Kanzlei not only provided vital intelligence for the Austrian government, it also sold information on to other European governments. For 1,000 ducats, the French embassy in Vienna received packages from the Geheime Kabinets-Kanzlei twice a week. When the first package was returned to Louis XV, he found dispatches from the King of Prussia to his spies in Vienna and Paris, as well as his own secret correspondence which had been deciphered.

The success of the Black Chambers forced cipher secretaries to change over to the more secure Vignère cipher.

In the 18th and 19th centuries most European capitals had their Black Chambers where encrypted mail was decrypted and read.

CHAPTER 4

BREAKING THE UNBREAKABLE

'A very simple arithmetic process may effectually conceal the meaning of a message from everyone but the persons who hold the key to the cipher. . . . the simpler the cipher, provided it is effectual, the better.'

Pliny Earle Chase,
American scientist and mathematician,
1820–86

The 19th century saw a vast expansion in communication. The United States spanned a continent and Britain had a worldwide empire. The invention of the telegraph provided a new way to transmit sensitive information long distances; but it could easily be tapped. New codes and methods of codebreaking were required.

Hieroglyphics like these, carved in the wall of the Deir El-Bahri Temple in Luxor, remained unreadable until the discovery of the Rosetta Stone. Many of the techniques devised by those deciphering long-dead languages were applied to codebreaking.

Morse code was first used to send messages down telegraph wires, then by wireless transmissions.

Breaking *le chiffre indéchiffrable*

By the middle of the 19th century, the electric telegraph was spreading across the USA and Europe. Messages were sent in Morse code, but this was not a form of encryption. It simply represented the letters of the alphabet as dots and dashes which could easily be sent along a telegraph cable as shorter and longer bursts of electrical current. Anyone who knew Morse code could read any unencoded message sent using it.

It was far from secure, because telegraph operators at both ends of the line got to read the message. Consequently, private or secret messages had to be encoded before they were handed to the telegraph clerk. Again,

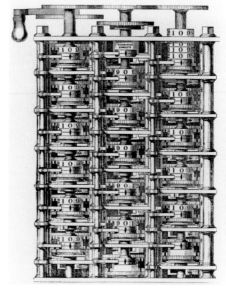

Part of Babbage's difference engine.

the best option was to use the Vigenère cipher. The race was on to break it.

One of those involved was Charles Babbage (see box below), the mathematician famous for his attempt to build a mechanical computer. Although his Analytical Engine was never completed, it was the forerunner of an electronic version used to crack codes in World War II.

An enthusiast for ciphers since boyhood, Babbage decoded the shorthand of the first Astronomer Royal, John Flamsteed, and the encoded notes of Charles I's wife, Henrietta Maria, and he lent his expertise in legal cases. Along the way he collected ciphers and planned to publish *The Philosophy of Decyphering*, another project he never finished.

A new cipher?

In 1854, a dentist from Bristol named John Hall Brock Thwaites wrote to the *Journal of the Society of Arts*, claiming to have invented a new cipher. Babbage pointed out that it was just a version of the Vigenère cipher. Thwaites then challenged Babbage to decode a sample he had enciphered, and Babbage did so. The plaintext was the poem 'The Vision of Sin' by Alfred Tennyson, encoded with the key word 'Emily', the name of Tennyson's wife.

CHARLES BABBAGE (1791–1871)

While still in his early twenties, Babbage made a small calculator that could perform certain mathematical computations to eight decimal places. Finding numerous errors in the newly calculated navigation tables in the *Nautical Almanac*, Babbage exclaimed: 'I wish to God these calculations had been executed by steam.' After impressing the Royal Society with an experimental prototype, Babbage set about designing a machine that could compute up to 20 decimal places and received British government funds to build it. He spent ten years working on his Difference Engine No. 1, only to abandon it and design an improved Difference Engine No 2. Then the government funding dried up. As Lucasian Professor of Mathematics at Cambridge University, Babbage began work on his Analytical Engine, which was to be programmable, receiving instructions from punched cards. It had a central processor and a memory – the basic elements of a modern computer. Babbage also helped set up the modern postal system in Britain, compiled the first reliable actuarial tables and invented a speedometer and a railway engine cow-catcher.

THE KASISKI EXAMINATION

Kasiski suggested looking for repeated fragments in the ciphertext and making a list of the distances that separate the repetitions. For example:

plaintext	T	o	b	e	o	r	n	o	t	t	o	b	e	t	h	a	t	i	s	t	h	e	q	u	e	s	t	i	o	n
key	K	E	Y	K	E	Y	K	E	Y	K	E	Y	K	E	Y	K	E	Y	K	E	Y	K	E	Y	K	E	Y	K	E	Y
ciphertext	D	S	Z	O	S	P	X	S	R	D	S	Z	O	X	F	K	X	G	C	X	F	O	U	S	O	w	R	S	S	L

Every time the 'to be' is enciphered by the letters KEYK, the repeated DSZO appears in the ciphertext. There is also a repeated XF where the 'th' of 'that' and 'the' are enciphered by EY. While it is possible for different combinations to appear by chance as the same sequence of letters in the ciphertext, it is far more common for regular combinations, such as the 't', 'h' and 'e' of 'the', to be enciphered by the same letter of the key.

Babbage never explained how he did this, perhaps because Britain had just embarked on the Crimean War so the ability to break the enemy's codes without their knowledge was vital. However, examination of his notes indicated that he had used a method developed independently by Prussian officer Friedrich Wilhelm Kasiski (see box opposite).

Babbage and Kasiski had both noticed that in Vigenère ciphertext, sequences of letters are often repeated. In the example given above, the key is just three letters long, so every third letter of the ciphertext is enciphered by the same line of the Vigenère square, which is a simple monoalphabetic substitution alphabet. So the polyalphabetic cipher given by the Vigenère square is, in

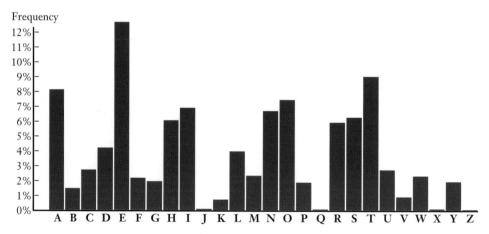

The frequency table showing the average occurrence of each letter in a body of English text.

fact, a number of monoalphabetic ciphers interwoven, each of which could be broken by frequency analysis.

However, as the encryption here is achieved using Caesar shifts, we can count the number of times each letter occurs in each of the three monoalphabetic ciphers and compare it to the standard frequency distribution in English. As well as the spike at 'e', there is a hump at 'r', 's' and 't', with distinct troughs before and after. By matching these to the spikes and humps in the distribution of letters in each of the three monoalphabetic ciphers, you can work out which line of the Vigenère square has been used to encipher it. Once you have all three you have the key, and the code can be broken.

Kasiski outlined this method in *Die Geheimschriften und die Dechiffrir-kunst* (*Secret Writing and the Art of Deciphering*) in 1863. The technique is still known as the Kasiski examination.

The Playfair cipher

The cipher which bears the name of scientist and politician Lord Playfair was in fact the

invention of his friend, the scientist and inventor Charles Wheatstone. But it was Playfair who promoted it by demonstrating it at a dinner in 1854 given by Lord President of the Council Earl Granville, whose guests included Prince Albert and

Charles Wheatstone.

FRIEDRICH WILHELM KASISKI (1805–81)

Born in Schlochau in West Prussia (now Człuchów in Poland), Friedrich Kasiski joined East Prussia's 33rd Infantry regiment at the age of 17. He retired with the rank of major 29 years later. However, he continued to serve in a territorial regiment until 1868, while devoting his spare time to cryptology. After the publication of *Die Geheimschriften und die Dechiffrir-kunst* in 1863, he lost interest in codebreaking and became an amateur anthropologist, excavating prehistoric graves with Danzig's Natural Science Society. Kasiski's technique was described in a chapter called 'The Decipherment of French Writing'. His book was dedicated to General Albrecht von Roon, Prussian minister of war. Three years after the book's publication, Prussia won a quick victory over Austria in the Seven Weeks' War and humbled France in the Franco-Prussian War four years after that.

the future prime minister Lord Palmerston.

To illustrate the use of Wheatstone's cipher at Granville's dinner, Playfair constructed a quick keysquare using PALMERSTON as the keyword.

P	A	L	M	E
R	S	T	O	N
B	C	D	F	G
H	I/J	K	Q	U
V	W	X	Y	Z

To encipher a message, the plaintext is divided into letter pairs or bigrams. So 'halt the attacks' becomes 'ha lt th ea tx ta ck sx'. If a letter is repeated consecutively (such as the double 't' in 'attacks'), an 'x' is inserted between the two letters. If a single letter appears at the end, an 'x' is added after this.

The encipherment is performed using the following rules. If both letters appear on the same row, they are each replaced by the letter to the right, so 'bd' becomes 'CF'. If one of the letters falls at the end of the row it is replaced by the one at the beginning, so 'dg' becomes 'FB'. If both letters appear in the same column, they are replaced by the letter beneath each one, so 'ld' becomes 'TK'. And if one of the letters occurs at the bottom of the column, it is replaced by the one at the top, so 'xt' is replaced by 'LD'.

If the two letters are neither in the same row nor the same column, take the first letter and follow the row until it intersects with the column where the second letter falls and use the letter that lies at the intersection. Then follow along the row where the second letter falls to the column where the first letter lies, and use the letter at that intersection. So 'ha lt th ea tx ta ck sx' becomes 'IP TD RK PL DL SL DI TW'. Reverse the process to decipher the message.

There are many advantages to this system. In any message, there are half as many bigrams as letters, so there are fewer elements available to decipher by frequency analysis. The most widely used letters in English, 'e' and 't', have average frequencies of 12 and 9 per cent, while the most common bigrams, 'th' and 'he', only have frequencies of 3¼ and 2½ per cent. And while there are only 26 letters, there are 676 bigrams.

When Playfair and Wheatstone explained this cipher to an undersecretary at the Foreign Office, he complained that it was too complicated. Wheatstone then offered to show that he could teach boys from the nearest elementary school how to use it in 15 minutes. 'That is very possible,' said the undersecretary, 'but you could never teach it to attachés.'

It is not clear whether the Playfair code was used during the Crimean War, but it was in the Boer War. In 1914, Lieutenant Joseph I. Mauborgne of the US Army Signal Corps published a solution to it. He pointed out that despite the lower frequency of bigrams,

> 'One of the most singular characteristics of the art of deciphering is the strong conviction possessed by every person, even moderately acquainted with it, that he is able to construct a cipher which nobody else can decipher. I have also observed that the cleverer the person, the more intimate is his conviction.'
>
> Charles Babbage, *Passages from the Life of a Philosopher*, 1864

these elements were still vulnerable to frequency analysis. Another weakness of the Playfair cipher is that the common bigrams 're' and 'er', and 'de' and 'ed' encipher into equivalent bigrams with the letter reversed, so if 're' becomes 'AB', 'er' becomes 'BA'.

Even though it had been broken, the Playfair cipher continued to be used in tactical communications as it was quick and easy to encipher and decipher, but time-consuming to crack. So, by the time the enemy had read the message in plaintext, the situation on the battlefield would have moved on and the intelligence gleaned would no longer be of use.

During the Boer Wars, the Wheatstone/Playfair code was used for military communications.

THE VOYNICH MANUSCRIPT

Some 240 pages of handwritten script in an unidentified cipher, the Voynich manuscript has defied decoding for centuries. The first record of it was in the court of the Holy Roman Emperor Rudolf II, patron of the astronomers Johannes Kepler and Tycho Brahe, who had purchased it for 600 ducats. On his abdication in 1611, the manuscript passed to Rudolf's botanist, Jacobus de Tepenec, then to the rector of Prague University, Johannes Marcus Marci. On 19 August 1666, Marci sent it to Athanasius Kircher, a Jesuit scholar who had recently published a book on cryptology, and boasted that he had solved the riddle of hieroglyphics. Marci's accompanying letter recalled that a former owner of the manuscript

The Voynich Manuscript still defies decryption.

had sent Kircher a portion of the text for decoding. Marci also wrote that the manuscript was believed to have been written by Roger Bacon (see box on page 57). Nothing is known of what became of the manuscript until 1912, when it was bought by American rare book dealer Wilfrid Voynich from the Jesuit school in Frascati, Italy. Voynich generously provided photocopies to anyone who wanted to try to decode it. In the 1920s, Professor Newbold of the University of Pennsylvania claimed to have cracked it. Following his death, his notes proved he had not. Codebreakers from both world wars tried and failed. The manuscript now resides at Yale.

The Beale Papers

Some ciphers have never been broken. One is the Voynich manuscript (see above), which probably dates from the 16th century. Another was described by James B. Ward of Lynchburg, Virginia, in a pamphlet entitled *The Beale Papers*, published in 1885. Ward told of his friend, Robert Morriss, proprietor of the Washington Hotel in Lynchburg, who had given him enciphered papers concerning the whereabouts of buried treasure.

According to the *Papers*, Morriss became acquainted with Thomas J. Beale

in January 1820, when he checked into the Washington. Beale was with two other gentlemen, who left for their homes in Richmond after a week or ten days. Beale stayed on until the end of March, at which point his two friends turned up again; then the three men left together.

Beale returned in January 1822. Before he left later that spring, he handed Morriss a box which he said contained important papers. Later, Morriss received a letter from Beale, mailed in St Louis, Missouri, and dated 9 May 1822 (see opposite page).

BEALE'S LETTER TO MORRISS

'With regard to the box left in your charge, I have a few words to say, and, if you will permit me, give you some instructions concerning it. It contains papers vitally affecting the fortunes of myself and many others engaged in business with me, and in the event of my death, its loss might be irreparable. You will, therefore, see the necessity of guarding it with vigilance and care to prevent so great a catastrophe. It also contains some letters addressed to yourself, and which will be necessary to enlighten you concerning the business in which we are engaged. Should none of us ever return you will please preserve carefully the box for the period of ten years from the date of this letter, and if I, or no one with authority from me during that time demands its restoration, you will open it, which can be done by removing the lock. You will find, in addition to the papers addressed to you, other papers which will be unintelligible without the aid of a key to assist you. Such a key I have left in the hands of a friend in this place, sealed, addressed to yourself, and endorsed not to be delivered until June, 1832. By means of this you will understand fully all you will be required to do.'

Neither Beale nor his friends ever turned up, nor did the letter containing the key. In 1845, Morriss finally got round to opening the box. Inside he found three sheets containing unintelligible numbers, plus two letters addressed to him. The first

told how Beale and his companions had, in April 1817, set out across the Western plains. After wintering in Santa Fe, they had headed out to follow an immense herd of buffalo. Making camp in a ravine some 300 miles to the north, they discovered gold.

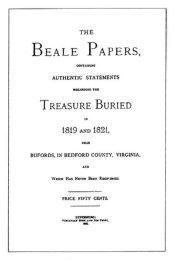

THE

BEALE PAPERS,

CONTAINING

AUTHENTIC STATEMENTS

REGARDING THE

TREASURE BURIED

IN

1819 AND 1821,

NEAR

BUFORDS, IN BEDFORD COUNTY, VIRGINIA,

AND

WHICH HAS NEVER BEEN RECOVERED.

PRICE FIFTY CENTS.

LYNCHBURG:
VIRGINIAN BOOK AND JOB PRINT.,
1885.

Despite being published as a 50-cent pamphlet so anyone could try cracking it, the sheets revealing the whereabouts of Beale's treasure remain unbroken.

Buried treasure

By the summer of 1819, they had accumulated so much gold that they decided it should be stored in some safe place. After some discussion, it was decided that Beale and a party should take it and bury it in a cave near Buford's tavern in Bedford County, Virginia, a place they all knew. They also decided that Beale should find someone trustworthy to apportion the treasure among their relatives should some disaster befall them.

Beale returned westwards, saying that he had found just such a person – Morriss.

The next autumn, he returned to Virginia with more precious metal, which he hid with the rest.

The first letter which had been addressed to Morriss continued as follows: 'As ten years must elapse before you will see this letter, you may well conclude by that time that the worst has happened, and that none of us are to be numbered with the living. In such an event, you will please visit the place of deposit and secure its contents, which you will divide into thirty-one equal parts; one of these parts you are to retain as your own, freely given to you for your services.'

The second letter said that one of the three papers, written in cipher, contained the names of all Beale's associates, along with the names and addresses of their relatives – but no cipher key was included. Morriss tried to decipher the three sheets, but failed. In 1862, aged 84, Morriss confided in Ward, who set to work deciphering the sheets. Ward succeeded in cracking the second sheet. It was written in a version of book code, known as a Beale cipher.

In a book code, the sender and recipient agree on a text, usually a book, then they number the words. The plaintext is encoded

---

THE BEALE CIPHER

The Beale cipher, named after Thomas J. Beale, uses a version of the book code that employs only the initial letter of words. Ward found that the second sheet was enciphered using the Declaration of Independence, or at least an early edition of it which used the world 'unalienable' instead of 'inalienable'. The pamphlet gave his workings:

When(1) in(2) the(3) course(4) of(5) human(6) events(7) it(8) becomes(9) necessary(10) for(11) one(12) people(13) to(14) dissolve(15) the(16) political(17) bands(18) which(19) have(20) connected(21) them(22) with(23) another(24) and(25) to(26) assume(27) among(28) the(29) powers(30) of(31) the(32) earth(33) the(34) separate(35) and(36) equal(37) station(38) to(39) which(40) the(41) laws(42) of(43) nature(44) and(45) of(46) nature's(47) god(48) entitle(49) them(50) a(51) decent(52) respect(53) to(54) the(55) opinions(56) of(57) mankind(58) requires(59) that(60) they(61) should(62) declare(63) the(64) causes(65) which(66) impel(67) them(68) to(69) the(70) separation(71) we(72) hold(73) these(74) truths(75) to(76) be(77) self(78) evident(79) that(80) all(81) men(82) are(83) created(84) equal(85) that(86) they(87) are(88) endowed(89) by(90) their(91) creator(92) with(93) certain(94) unalienable(95) rights(96) that(97) among(98) these(99) are(100) life(101) liberty(102) and(103) the(104) pursuit(105) of(106) happiness(107)

So 1 = w; 2 = i; 3 = t; 4 = c; 5 = o; 6 = h; 7 = e; 8 = i, and so on. As more than one number can stand for each letter, the quantity depending on the text, the cipher cannot be broken by frequency analysis.

Beale and his companions wintered in Santa Fe before heading out after buffalo – and finding gold.

using the number of each word. However, if the word does not appear in the text, it cannot be encoded. To overcome this problem, a dictionary can be used, but the numbers become unwieldy. Ward's rendering of sheet two was:

'I have deposited in the county of Bedford, about four miles from Buford's, in an excavation or vault, six feet below the surface of the ground, the following articles, belonging jointly to the parties whose names are given in number '3', herewith: The first deposit consisted of one thousand and fourteen pounds of gold, and three thousand eight hundred and twelve pounds of silver, deposited November, 1819. The second was made December, 1821, and consisted of nineteen hundred and seven pounds of gold, and twelve hundred and eighty-eight pounds of silver; also jewels, obtained in St. Louis in exchange for silver to save transportation, and valued at $13,000. The above is securely packed in iron pots, with iron covers. The vault is roughly lined with stone, and the vessels rest on solid stone, and are covered with others. Paper number 1 describes the exact locality of the vault so that no difficulty will be had in finding it.'

'There is a message in those codes. If it turns out to be something like, "April Fool Sucker," so what? If Tommy Beale has been playing a trick on me, I've come out ahead, because the whole affair has been fascinating and just plain fun.'

Dr Carl Hammer, 1964

In the years following Beale's disappearance, the western states of North America witnessed a gold rush.

The treasure would be worth $30 million today, but Ward couldn't crack sheet one so didn't find it. He spent 23 years on the task, reducing himself to penury in the process. In 1885, he finally gave up and published a pamphlet containing the enciphered sheets, giving others a chance to try their hand.

Would-be codebreakers have tried to solve the sheets – using the United States Constitution, the Bible, the plays of Shakespeare and numerous other texts. The ciphers were also sent to the Riverbank Laboratories of George Fabyan in Geneva, Illinois, where America's military cryptography was carried out during World War I. But cryptanalysts there also failed to break them.

The best minds in America

In 1964, Dr Carl Hammer, director of computer sciences at Sperry Univac, went to work on the enciphered papers, using the company's new computer. Although he failed to crack the cipher, his analysis of sheet one showed that it had been encrypted in the same way as sheet two (the sheet Ward had broken). 'We have played games with these numbers that would take a million men and a billion years to duplicate with pen and paper,' he said. 'We have searched out just about every scrap of the historical record that might give us a clue. A number of us have been over the ground, although I am convinced that cryptanalysis is the only fruitful line of attack.' Hammer remained convinced that the code was breakable. He estimated that his efforts to crack the code had engaged at least 10 per cent of the best cryptanalytic minds in America and the work they had put in exceeded the value of the treasure.

ROGER BACON (1220–92)

The first known European book to describe the use of cryptography was written by English Franciscan monk and polymath Roger Bacon. An early proponent of experimental science, he studied mathematics, astronomy, optics, alchemy and language, proposing such advanced idea as aeroplanes, motorized ships, horseless carriages, microscopes and telescopes, and he was the first European to detail the process of making gunpowder. In his *Epistle on the Secret Works of Art and the Nullity of Magic*, he outlined seven methods for keeping messages secret, using such techniques as exotic alphabets, shorthand and symbols invented by the author. 'A man is crazy who writes a secret in any other way than one which will conceal it from the vulgar,' he cautioned. He was at one time believed to be the author of the Voynich manuscript.

As well as being a Franciscan monk, Roger Bacon was a philosopher, educational reformer, proponent of experimental science and cryptographer.

CHAPTER 5

ROOM 40

'*About a fortnight later the Commandant sent for me and silently handed me a War Office telegram: "Lieutenant-Interpreter Toye is to report as soon as possible to the Admiralty for special duty." So omnipotent and expeditious is the British Admiralty when its mind is once made up; think of the yards of red tape that must have been cut in those two weeks!*'

Frank Toye,
codebreaker, Room 40

During World War I, radio took over as a more flexible means of communication, but radio messages were even easier to intercept than those sent by telegraph. The British set up a network of listening posts, intercepting official German messages which were sent back to the Admiralty to be decrypted.

The Admiralty building in Whitehall was home to a team dedicated to breaking the German naval codes in World War I.

Radio communication

The invention of the telegraph was followed at the turn of the 20th century by an even more insecure means of communication – radio. Nevertheless, to the military the advantages of using radio were obvious. Messages could be transmitted instantly between locations without the need for telegraph wires. This allowed army units a new freedom to manoeuvre. Navies also took up the new invention as it enabled ships to stay in communication even though they were out of the line of sight. The obvious problem was that any message broadcast over the airwaves could easily be intercepted; this meant that safer and more secure codes and ciphers were needed.

World War I

Before dawn on 5 August 1914, the day after Britain had declared war on Germany, the British cable ship *Telconia* tore up Germany's transatlantic cables. This was Britain's first offensive action of the war. It ensured that enemy messages to the USA would be sent by radio or via another nation's telegraph cables; the messages would then pass through a relay station at Porthcurno near Land's End, where copies could be made.

Later that day, Rear Admiral Henry Oliver, the director of naval intelligence, had lunch with the director of naval education, Sir Alfred Ewing, who had an interest in cryptology. Oliver already had a stack of

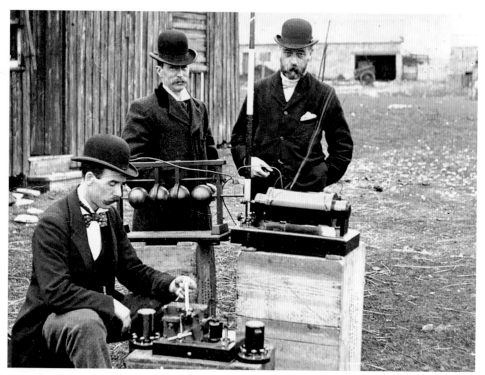

British Post Office engineers inspect Guglielmo Marconi's wireless telegraphy (radio) equipment in 1897.

THE EIGHTH WONDER OF THE WORLD.
THE ATLANTIC CABLE.

Laying the Atlantic cable, 'the Eighth Wonder of the World', in 1858.

intercepts piling up on his desk. Ewing immediately recognized them as German naval signals. If they could be decoded, the information garnered would be of vital importance.

Ewing began researching ciphers in the reading rooms of the British Museum, at Lloyd's of London and at the General Post Office, where commercial codes (coded abbreviations devised so businesses could save on the cost of cables) were kept on file. He recruited four German speakers who were teachers at naval colleges at Osborne and Dartmouth to help in decrypting them.

A friend of Ewing's named Russell Clarke, an amateur radio enthusiast who had supplied some of the intercepts, set up a listening station at Hunstanton on the Norfolk coast. This was the beginning of the Y Service, eventually comprising 14 listening stations that intercepted almost all official German messages. These were fed back to the Admiralty by landline.

At first, Ewing's team made little progress. All they had to go on was a signal book taken from a German steamer seized off Melbourne, Australia on 11 August. It was of little help. Then they got lucky.

Hunstanton lighthouse – a former listening station.

found still clutching the German naval codebooks. The Russians offered the books to their allies, the British, then the world's leading naval power; the First Lord of the Admiralty Winston Churchill sent a ship to collect them.

The codebooks didn't enable Ewing's team to decipher German messages immediately. Fleet Paymaster and principal German expert Charles Rotter soon realized that the messages had been coded, then super-enciphered (enciphered again) using simple monoalphabetic substitution. This made them easy to break, as certain code words were used more frequently than others and appeared in recognized clusters.

On 26 August, the German light cruiser SMS *Magdeburg* ran aground in the Gulf of Finland. The Russian Navy picked up the body of a drowned officer, who was

Intelligence Division Section 25

Ewing's team expanded quickly to handle the amount of traffic that was now being intercepted. In November 1914, they were moved into Room 40 of the Old Buildings

Codebooks taken from the light cruiser SMS Magdeburg *helped British codebreakers in their first attempts to crack the German naval codes.*

of the Admiralty, on the same corridor as the First Sea Lord. Adjoining their office was a small room equipped with a camp bed, where overworked cipher clerks could rest. The unit was later officially designated Section 25 of the Intelligence Division, or ID25, but the name Room 40 stuck even when the codebreakers moved into larger premises.

The unit then had another stroke of luck. A British trawler had brought up a lead-lined box of papers jettisoned by a German torpedo boat which had been sunk during the Battle of Texel on 17 October 1914.

The listening stations masqueraded as direction-finding units, so the Germans would not know that their signal traffic was being monitored. On 14 December 1914, the codebreakers of Room 40 discovered that a raiding party from the German Imperial Navy was coming out of port to attack British coastal towns. Royal Navy ships were sent, but not to intercept the German Navy, as this would have given the game away; instead, their objective was to cut the German flotilla off from port and engage it on its return from bombarding its targets – the towns of Hartlepool and Scarborough. It meant the naval high command had to accept the inevitable civilian deaths from the attack rather than reveal that they had broken the German naval code. As it turned out, the Royal Navy lost the German raiders in fog.

Bombardment of Scarborough: Germany in Desperation Attacks our Defenceless Coast Town

The naval bombardment of Hartlepool and Scarborough made the interception of the German High Seas Fleet vital.

63

The German High Seas Fleet left port again on 23 January 1915 to reconnoitre the Dogger Bank. The Royal Navy employed the same tactics as before, but this time managed to intercept the raiders, sinking one cruiser and badly damaging two others. The reputation of Room 40 was now secured and the number of analysts there was boosted to 50.

Although the German fleet didn't venture out of port again for a year, in February 1915 they changed the cipher key. But the codebreakers of Room 40 were now familiar with the code words and the new cipher was quickly broken. Winston Churchill visited their office to congratulate them.

By 1916, instead of changing the key every three months, the German Navy was changing it every night at midnight. By then the codebreakers of Room 40 were so adept that they sometimes broke it as early as 2 a.m., but almost certainly by 10 a.m.

Columnar transposition

After the Battle of Jutland in June 1916, the Germans mainly relied on their U-boats to attack the British. They used the same code book, but then enciphered again (super-encipherment) by means of columnar transposition.

> 'I first realized what an unusual brain Alan had when he presented me with a paper on the reaction between iodic acid and sulphur dioxide. . . he had worked out the mathematics of it in a way that astonished me.'
>
> Alan Turing's school science master,
> A.J.P. Andrews, 1930

To scramble letters using columnar transposition, the message is written out in rows of a length fixed by the keyword. If the message 'attack British fleet at dawn tomorrow' is enciphered using the keyword UBOATS, the grid is drawn up as follows:

U	B	O	A	T	S
a	t	t	a	c	k
b	r	i	t	i	s
h	f	l	e	e	t
a	t	d	a	w	n
t	o	m	o	r	r
o	w	j	q	r	w

The remaining boxes in the last line are filled out with nulls. The columns are then transposed, following the alphabetical order of the keyword (ABOSTU):

A	B	O	S	T	U
a	t	t	k	c	a
t	r	i	s	i	b
e	f	l	t	e	h
o	t	d	n	w	a
o	o	m	r	r	t
q	w	j	w	r	o

The message is then sent reading column by column, so the transmitted text is:

ATEOOQ TRFTOW TILDMJ KSTNRW CIEWRR ABHATO

Removing the nulls produces enciphered text of unequal lengths, which makes it easier to crack. To decrypt, you reverse the process – a straightforward task, if you have the keyword.

To confuse the codebreakers further, the message can be enciphered twice, using the same keyword or a different one. The German Navy did not do this, as they were already enciphering coded text.

To tighten security, the Germans changed their codebook in August 1916. But, on the night of 23 September, Zeppelin L32 was shot down over Essex, killing all 22 members of the crew. A charred copy of the new codebook was recovered from the wreckage. Another copy was recovered by a diver from a U-boat sunk off the coast of Kent. So the codebreakers of Room 40 could carry on as before.

The Zimmermann telegram

One of the key events of World War I was the decoding of the Zimmermann telegram, sent on 16 January 1917 by German Foreign Secretary Arthur Zimmermann to the German embassy in Washington, D.C.

From there, it was to be forwarded to the German legation in Mexico City.

In an attempt to starve Britain into submission, the Germans planned to resume unrestricted submarine warfare, which risked bringing the United States into the war on the Allies' side. In this event, Germany proposed an alliance with Mexico, offering generous financial support to help it reconquer its lost territories of Texas, Arizona and New Mexico. American troops would be tied down there, rather than sent to the Western Front in Europe, and supplies being sent to the Western Allies would be diverted.

The encrypted telegram was sent via Sweden, with a back-up handed to the US Embassy in Berlin to be sent via an American-owned cable. Both cables passed through the relay station at Porthcurno, so copies soon found their way on to the desks of the codebreakers in Room 40.

A charred copy of a codebook was rescued from the wreckage of Zeppelin L32, shot down over Essex on 23 September 1916, as shown in this newspaper photograph.

The message was encoded using German naval code 0075, comprising 10,000 words and phrases numbered 0000 to 9999 in a random order. The British already had codebooks for 0075; they were among those retrieved from the SMS *Magdeburg* by the Russians in 1914. The Zimmermann telegram had been super-enciphered (encoded again using the diplomatic cipher 13040), but this did not disguise the underlying code, which was in groups of three, four and five digits.

When Germany's ambassador to the USA protested to Berlin about the resumption of unrestricted submarine warfare (as he was doing his utmost to keep America out of the war) the Admiralty codebreakers soon found they had other super-enciphered messages. With more material to work on, the codebreakers began to identify the word 'stop', which appeared regularly in telegrams, and diplomatic phrases such as 'Your Excellency'. Within a day, they had partially broken the code – enough to show the momentous significance of the telegram.

By 5 February, they had decoded it completely. The question was, what to do with it? The British could not reveal that they were able to break the German code, nor could they admit to tapping US cable traffic or that of other neutrals.

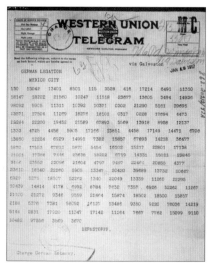

Cracking the code of the Zimmermann telegram brought America into the war.

However, with a little judicial bribery, the British ambassador in Mexico managed to obtain another copy of the telegram. This was the one that the German embassy in Washington, D.C. had forwarded to Mexico City, where they did not have the 0075 code. So it had been re-enciphered using only the older diplomatic cipher 13040.

While proclaiming to the world that they had stolen a copy of the deciphered text in Mexico, the British showed the 13040 version to the US government, which they could check with their own cable intercepts. As a result, the English translation of the cable was published in American newspapers and, on 6 April 1917, the United States declared war on Germany.

German field ciphers

Knowing that radio messages could easily be overheard, the Germans developed new ciphers throughout World War I. The most famous was the ADFGVX cipher, which was developed from the earlier ADFGX cipher. It was introduced on 5 March 1918, immediately before the launch of the German Spring Offensive, which aimed to defeat the Allies before American troops arrived on the Western Front in any significant numbers.

THE ADFGVX CIPHER

The ADFGVX cipher uses two-part encipherment. The Polybius square has six rows and six columns which are designated using the six letters. The square is then filled out with the 26 letters of the alphabet and the ten digits from 0 to 9.

	A	D	F	G	V	X
A	g	v	z	j	c	n
D	s	b	8	q	t	e
F	4	p	h	a	x	i
G	l	1	m	2	5	u
V	w	f	6	y	0	d
X	r	3	k	7	o	9

To encipher the message 'attack at 0800', we get:

a	t	t	a	c	k	a	t	0	8	0	0
FG	DV	DV	FG	AV	XF	FG	DV	VV	DF	VV	VV

This is a monoalphabetic cipher which could be cracked using frequency analysis, so it is enciphered a second time by columnar transposition, this time using the keyword BANG:

B	A	N	G
F	G	D	V
D	V	F	G
A	V	X	F
F	G	D	V
V	V	D	F
V	V	V	V

This is then re-arranged alphabetically:

A	B	G	N
G	F	V	D
V	D	G	F
V	A	F	X
G	F	V	D
V	V	F	D
V	V	V	V

So the enciphered message to be transmitted reads: GVVGVVFDAFVVVGFVFVDFXDDV

The ciphers took their names from the letters that appeared in the cryptograms. These letters were chosen because they were the most distinct in Morse code and thus the least likely to be misread:

A   . —
D   — . .
F   . . — .
G   — — .
V   . . . —
X   — . . —

Lieutenant Georges Painvin

In the spring of 1918, at the French Bureau de Chiffre, Lieutenant Georges Painvin set to work breaking the ADFGVX code. He had cut his teeth on the earlier ADFGX code, which didn't include the letter 'J' or the numbers. The use of just five letters suggested a Polybius square had been used. But Painvin couldn't decipher the code using frequency analysis. This mean it was not a simple monoalphabetic substitution. Painvin reasoned that a polyalphabetic code was too cumbersome to be used in the field, so guessed that transposition had been used.

Military messages adopt a fairly standard form. Consequently, it was reasonable to assume that the same words or phrases enciphered using the same Polybius square and the same keyword had been enciphered in the same way. Noting the repetitions, Painvin could guess the length of the columns. He noted that in certain messages some of the enciphered groups included an extra letter. This was because the last line of the transposition square had fallen short and had not been filled out with nulls. The longer groups must therefore come from the left-hand side of the square, and the shorter groups from the right. It was then possible to guess the length of the keyword.

If the keyword contained an even number of letters, each column of the transposition table would consist either of letters from the top of the Polybius square or from down the side, but not a mix of the two. Painvin paired up top letters and side letters and performed frequency analysis on them. If he paired up the wrong columns the result would be flat, but pairing the right ones

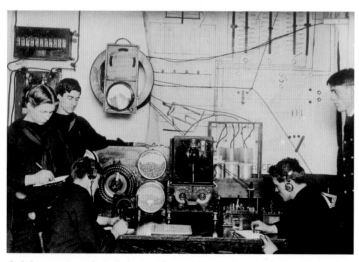

Coded messages sent by radio became the vital means of communication, particularly in wartime. Here a US Navy crew is drilled in the use of wireless communications on board ship during World War I.

would approximate to the standard distribution. From there, Painvin filled out the transposition block and deciphered the message. This took him 48 hours.

The extra V

On 1 June 1918, with the Germans just 30 miles from Paris, Painvin saw that the letter V had appeared in the code. He also noticed that three messages sent from the same transmitter were identical in length and assumed that the message was the same in each case. Only the addressee was different. The messages would all have been enciphered identically in the Polybius square, but the extra one or two letters in the address would move it along in the transposition block. Within an hour, he had cracked the ADFGVX code.

When the next German assault began, the French were ready. In fierce fighting, they managed to halt the enemy and save Paris. The war, which could have been lost by the Allies at that moment, was won a few months later.

Frequency and trigrams

By the end of World War I, the hunt was on for unbreakable codes. Clearly *le chiffre indéchiffrable* still had its place. The technique

A young Lieutenant George Painvin.

of Babbage and Kasiski would not work if the key was as long as the message itself. A passage from a book could be selected, for example, but even this was not secure. The word 'the' appears frequently in English, meaning that 't', 'h' and 'e' can be used repeatedly, working backwards from the ciphertext, to give three-letter groups in the key using the Vigenère square. Many trigrams could be discarded because they gave a combination, such as KQB, which was so rare as to be impossible. But the feasible trigrams could provide valuable clues.

The one-time pad

By 1918, Joseph Mauborgne, who had broken the Playfair code, had risen to become a US Army major and head of cryptographic research. He then discovered you could make *le chiffre indéchiffrable* secure again if you used a key the same length as the message and made up of a series of random letters. The same key letters would have to be used by sender and recipient and could only be used once, so this key is known as a one-time pad.

If two messages enciphered using the same one-time pad are intercepted, it may

PERSISTENCE PAYS OFF

In *The Code Book*, author Simon Singh gives an example of deciphering the following ciphertext:

VHRMHEUZNFQDEZRWXFIDK

He tests 'the' against arbitrary fragments of code and immediately comes up trumps. Testing 'the' against the first three-letter VHR gives the keyletters CAN, which are a perfectly feasible arrangement. Skipping the next three letters, he tries again with UZN, which yields BSJ – an unfeasible combination. Further along, he tries 'the' with the letters RWX. This gives the keyletters YPT. Though rare, this combination appears in APOCALYPTIC, CRYPT and EGYPT or derivatives of those words. It is then simply a matter of testing these possible keywords by using them to decipher that part of the ciphertext:

V	H	R	M	H	E	U	Z	N	F	Q	D	E	Z	R	W	X	F	I	D	K
C	A	N							A	P	O	C	A	L	Y	P	T	I	C	
t	h	e							n	q	c	b	e	o	t	h	e	x	g	

Clearly this does not work, as the plaintext makes no sense, so he tries again:

V	H	R	M	H	E	U	Z	N	F	Q	D	E	Z	R	W	X	F	I	D	K
C	A	N										C	R	Y	P	T				
t	h	e										c	i	t	h	e				

This doesn't work either. However, the following:

V	H	R	M	H	E	U	Z	N	F	Q	D	E	Z	R	W	X	F	I	D	K
C	A	N										E	G	Y	P	T				
t	h	e										a	t	t	h	e				

be possible to crack the code. The way to do it is to assume that the whole of the first message is made up of the word 'the'. Then it's possible to work backwards to come up with a first attempt at revealing the series of random letters which constitute the key. This can then be used to partially decipher the second message. Some small fragments of words may then emerge showing where the keytext is correct. Building from these fragments, in the same way as the example above, it's possible to deduce the whole of the random sequence.

If the one-time pad is used only once and then destroyed, the ciphertext it generated will be truly unbreakable – at least in theory. A message of 21 letters will need a keytext of 21 random letters to encrypt it. This

gives a piece of plaintext that does make sense. Perhaps the keytext is a list of countries? Maybe CAN is the beginning of CANADA? These deductions are tested, as follows:

V	H	R	M	H	E	U	Z	N	F	Q	D	E	Z	R	W	X	F	I	D	K
C	A	N	A	D	A							E	G	Y	P	T				
t	h	e	m	e	e							a	t	t	h	e				

It is reasonable to assume that 'mee' is the beginning of the word 'meeting'. When we try that out we get:

V	H	R	M	H	E	U	Z	N	F	Q	D	E	Z	R	W	X	F	I	D	K
C	A	N	A	D	A	B	R	A	Z			E	G	Y	P	T				
t	h	e	m	e	e	t	i	n	g			a	t	t	h	e				

It would be safe to assume that the second country here, starting BRAZ, is BRAZIL. Now we are looking for one more country to complete the key. There are only a limited number of countries with a name of just four letters. One of them, CUBA, gives:

V	H	R	M	H	E	U	Z	N	F	Q	D	E	Z	R	W	X	F	I	D	K
C	A	N	A	D	A	B	R	A	Z	I	L	E	G	Y	P	T	C	U	B	A
t	h	e	m	e	e	t	i	n	g	i	s	a	t	t	h	e	d	o	c	k

The cipher has been cracked.

means there will be 50 billion billion billion possible keys to test. Even if that were possible, you would never know whether you can come up with the right message, as testing every possible key would produce every possible combination of 21 letters in plaintext. The likelihood is that more than a handful of these would make sense in English, so you wouldn't be able to tell which was the correct message.

It's difficult to generate a truly random series of letters. The only way is to use machinery operated by the random decay of a radioactive element. If each one-time pad is destroyed after use, hundreds if not thousands would be required for use in a military situation. They would have to be distributed to all those sending and receiving messages, and everyone would have to use the same one at the same time. If the enemy managed to intercept a courier, the security of the system would be compromised and the cipher book would have to be scrapped and started again. Consequently, the one-time pad is only practical in limited situations – such as when a spy is sending a message back to his or her agency.

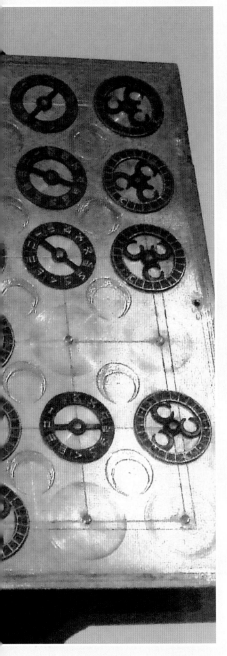

CHAPTER 6

THE BIRTH OF MECHANIZATION

'It will be absolutely impossible, even for one perfectly acquainted with the general system, ever to decypher the writing of another without his key.'

Professor Robert Patterson,
University of Pennsylvania

The mechanization of cryptography had begun with Alberti's cipher disc in the 15th century (see page 38). Although a version of this was still being used in the American Civil War, the third US president, Thomas Jefferson, invented another system in the 18th century. The US Army was still using a version of Jefferson's wheel cipher well into the 20th century.

A 16th-century French cipher machine concealed within a book.

Jefferson's disk cipher and (inset) the modern combination lock, which is based on this type of cipher.

Wheels within wheels

During the American Revolution (1765–83), Thomas Jefferson invented a simple mechanical device that enciphered messages. It consisted of 36 wooden disks with the letters of the alphabet arranged in random order around their edges. Each disc was different. The sender and recipient had to assemble the discs on an axle in an agreed order then rotate them until they spelled out a line of the message. Then another line from the cylinder, containing seemingly random letters, was recorded in the same way. Jefferson worked out that the number of possible arrangements of the wheels was 36 factorial (or 36 x 35 x 34 x 33 ... 4 x 3 x 2 x 1), which he calculated to be '372 with 39 cyphers [zeros] added to it' or 3.72×10^{41}. This outcome compares favourably with the three-rotor Enigma machine invented in Germany in the 1920s, which yields some 10^{23} combinations (see page 94).

Patterson's cipher

Jefferson didn't use his own cipher machine, preferring instead to use a nomenclator (a list of names that can be substituted one for another) devised by the US Secretary for Foreign Affairs Robert Livingston. As president of the United States, Jefferson (then also president of the American Philosophical Society) also recommended a system devised by Robert Patterson, professor of mathematics at the University of Pennsylvania. This was a simple columnar transposition with nulls at the heads of the columns, along with more nulls to fill out the line, but Patterson wrote: 'It will be absolutely impossible, even for one perfectly acquainted with the general system, ever to decypher the writing of another without his key.' Patterson estimated the number of keys to be 'ninety millions of millions'. Jefferson passed the cipher on to Livingston, who still preferred to stick with his nomenclator.

Patterson gave an example of how a message was to be encoded. The key, he said, was 58, 71, 33, 49, 83, 14, 62, 20. The first number gives the order of the lines, the second, the number of nulls which precede it. He proposed encoding the following:

Thomas Jefferson, US president and cryptographer.

'Buonaparte has at last given peace to Europe! France is now at peace with all the world. Four treaties have been concluded with the chief Consul within three weeks, to wit, with Portugal, Britain, Russia, and Turkey. A copy of the latter, which was signed at Paris on Friday, we received last night, in the French Journals to the nineteenth. The news was announced, at the Theatres on the sixteenth, and next day by the firing of cannon, and other demonstrations of joy.'

First draft:

1 binleihtsheeenaeear
2 uvclstihiedcfinsxna
3 oeethhnpalaernnotnt
4 nnihattoaatieeondoi
5 apsevhhrntpvntutano
6 penweertdtaecenhyan
7 aaoobceuterdhecebns
8 rcwreheguriljnesydo
1 tealeiwarwsaotditof
2 ettdneelkhosuhaxhtj
3 hopfcfebeintrttteho
4 aeeoockrycfnnhtefey
5 suaunosiahriaeheir
6 arcrcnttcwiglnenrd
7 toetlsoaoadhsettie
8 lpwruuwipsattwhhnm
1 aeiedlinysyioseago
2 sftaewtroiwntwanon
3 trhtdiwufgethatdfs
4 gaaiwtistnrhesrnct

Transcribed in cipher:

wsataispapsevhhrntpvntutano
eaaoobceuterdhecebnsbvatdepdno
chnoeethhnpalaernnotntutioh
nemeyeesannihattoaatieeondoi
rtlrcwreheguriljnesydothdsear
seeobinleihtsheeenaeeartanrm
arpenweertdtaecenhyanoabi
uvclstihiedcfinsxnahonylenrf

```
s d t r o d i e s u a u n o s i a h r i a e h e i r p
s t o e t l s o a o a d h s e t t i e u a h r d c i u y
f t s h o p t c f e b e i n t r t t t e h o r e o y p u
p o r t e r e p i a e e o o c k r y c f n n h t e f e y o
t l r l p w r u u w i p s a t t w h h n m e n t
e r r e t e a l e i w a r w s a o t d i t o f n g e
w h a r c r c n t t c w i g l n e n r d h f o w s h
e t t d n e e l k h o s u h a x h t j o r u i y i
s a u t r h t d i w u f g e t h a t d f s l t m
a d t r o d i i e g a a i w t i s t n r h e s r n C T
n o n o a e i e d l i n y s y i o s e a g o d l l m n
s f t a e w t r o i w n t w a n o n s y o u r c h
```

The first line in the transcription is line 5 from the first group in the draft and they are transcribed in the key order 5, 7, 3, 4, 8, 1, 6, 2, within the eight line groups. In the final four lines, they follow the same order 3, 4, 1, 2, ignoring the numbers above four. Then a random collection of letters is added at the beginning of the line

according to the second number in each pair of digits in the key – 8, 1, 3, 9, 3, 4, 2, 0. Patterson said: 'It will be proper that the supplementary letters, used at the beginning and end of the lines, should be nearly in the same relative proportion to each other in which they occur in the cypher itself, so that no clue may be afforded for distinguishing between them and the significant letters.' Patterson's letter included an enciphered message, with no key, which he challenged Jefferson to crack, saying: 'I shall conclude this paper with a specimen of secret writing, which I may safely defy the united ingenuity of the whole human race to decypher, to the end of time – but which, however, by the help of the key, consisting of not more than eighteen figures, might be read, with the utmost ease, in less than fifteen minutes:

Claude Chappe's optical telegraph.

CLAUDE CHAPPE (1763–1805)

In 1792, French inventor Claude Chappe demonstrated a semaphore system, the first practical telecommunications system of the industrial age. For almost 50 years, optical telegraphs became part of the landscape in Europe and can be spotted in the background of many paintings from this period. They are also mentioned in novels and poems. Victor Hugo, for instance, wrote a long poem called *Le Télégraphe*, and Chappe's semaphore figures prominently in Alexandre Dumas' *The Count of Monte Cristo*. The first official message to be sent via this system reported the recapture of the city of Le Quesnoy from the Austrians and the Prussians. In 1799 Napoleon seized power and used an optical telegraph to send the message: 'Paris is quiet and the good citizens are content.'

bonirnrsewehaipohiluoeettiseesnhiestctfhuesraeas
opiacdasthtaleeletubegtneinnfdecwebssssuifemsetnb
tfcabaenniaepatwethaharhefeisnueisutvaesdihfrsrniboi
kinrrgdvsconhsnheleltentngtsctlhshlbdpetguaistnjvtrscm
odneteitieedrebanirnnrhooifehtelstieisefcretcnuspecenr
bohsutirrsesolototamfyiysdhthiuhtloealobusiotntykjeetu
asesntdmeoatsbehracststnetmomrnosewdaneymnamcreseedoym
edneesemithfrtteaeaeeebttcfhdustslurisvucysiucremystvam
cohasefbsiesashtieadiiocftpricdnarswunhreshegitht
edaapthutheeaapueyeenlhhiemhniasaoaksienoimetesfsesaapnore
eevrslyedclnarcssndeetnreeensattciunngrrechhogaeecmrsreshy
nesvomethenetovrnnrrgeouhoeilamaitsgterewtnrttdmreiisrth
gbrhsearysuwebdrethetorpsgnspwcttebcnfgaiernuecfrnssamrnpsie
oeolgelsujntlncretpehdebtgvvotermrtndnehhitensimoeheootanp
psginhsataatoptwiugtedegiocteodftlnditrsogedttnwfsenrs
neaguatnadaedtlradhsvedspvlhyahdrrenachntcsvtsbtingfad
lonmnhxtednywsnfedtaysirrarersmngnnmbotititslrrrriswmyst
haebyhcstfhudnoeiltttnjtutnasdoggolrraahtouoanipstormno
oxoxiesnotnouahegropdeooptthcraehovugaienoauaadwot
zinmeerrolthoimeapcolhhomuwcomnhhvelremabeipcnimrahor
wshhurrierdeirssaohdatbtueihtleeeataieafgretdyotebuledsnnreer
gunnaaerceqtilnmeafeshtaedaaedyetsilmsrhineatmplmlxeerhh
raoitalonhmarirenraatpuvttrlpnoliaootnpvasttnonobprsnob
trihsseoiorpvnssntorropawworaaenelepthaeeidbnehssoemrri
pvlneuofseegtgshleenireefoyneenixooibsrreedmeaaftsmaaree
reertcohauunaweithnteilnolprfadhtnyutohesniierddmerei
stddiehvsnaeoctaooedcagnerrtriimstgpsrcuaadnesthhlapiorpi
esttdrctahtsueaoleoehacmpsoeeelgsimrlsnwfhdeisahtintvoumiu
lneabmopohtdfctrtteisahanzmssheeihsmbuenuoiilniprimci
motedtrhenponauearessrysoinsroaithhsooyghhlttablmnsrry
inaaopteecmocwtikeeeiehimoeisildgdnstynjuoapserriotimit
perervraadteotiswtdtaattrrnsftieetcuhadettranryynlf
axnyeflneiemaheohsnfnebgiopltrdgteestwtcasshassm
trsnomiieeinierwlnhrehrtuhmdhosknsreferucehdtotooguaa
inafpeeshshiuteontnsstwsttofeltgtunneoteabltueitoovsepr
smrnpnesdshediuqcetteosiupectahfmestdrsiwhffipcrsny
noiiueoeohfchehharisdogtadwyibstrecrvswonhihedtssrces
whfaairdegtvmhtmumttaecmsvsdtrodieshvuanoftsnfperre
ophrcvstoitrctueloecfitnoleanaesaueeofetetrnetyofssyst
supeinnuonsnnletheqisltfeanoinaetnlihwlcpiporterepiybst'

This message lay undeciphered in Jefferson's papers for over 200 years until it came to the attention of Lawren Smithline, a mathematician at the Center for Communications Research, a division of the Institute for Defense Analyses in Princeton, New Jersey.

Smithline realized that, while such a code was impervious to single-letter frequency analysis, he could break it using the frequency analysis of digraphs or bigrams. Using the 80,000 letters in Jefferson's State of the Union addresses, he made up a 26 x 26 table of the frequencies of aa, ab, ac,... ba, bb, bc,... zx, zy, zz. He used this table to evaluate which columns lay next to one another.

'For instance, the letter pair "vj" is impossible in English, so that excludes any alignment that creates that digraph,' Smithline said. 'Alternatively, the letter pair "qu" is rare, but when there is a "q," it must line up with a "u." When "q" and "u" do line up, that is strong evidence in favour of that alignment.'

Although he had modern computers at his disposal, Smithline was determined to use only those techniques available at the time. Mathematically, his statistical analysis had 'reduced the overall computational load to fewer than 100,000 simple sums – tedious in the nineteenth century, but doable'. He finally worked out the key in 2007, which was 13, 34, 57, 65, 22, 78, 49. The plaintext turned out to be the preamble to the Declaration of Independence which, of course, Jefferson had written. Also hidden away in Jefferson's papers in the Library of Congress were the details of the design of Jefferson's cipher wheel. These came to light in 1922.

Men work with telegraph ciphering equipment at the Telegraph and Cipher Bureau, 1903.

The Wadsworth cipher

US artillery officer and engineer Colonel Decius Wadsworth developed a mechanical method of enciphering in 1817. Like Alberti (see page 38), he had two sets of discs. The outer disc had the 26 letters of the alphabet, plus numbers 2–8. These were stamped on brass plugs that could be assembled in any order. The inner disc had only the 26 letters. The two discs were connected by gears with a ratio of 33:26. A small brass plate ran across the scales at the point where the two alphabets were in conjunction, and two holes revealed the equivalent letters.

The sender and recipient had to agree on the order of the letters on the outer ring

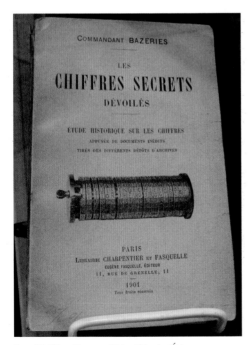

Les Chiffres Secrets Dévoilés, *by Étienne Bazeries, 1901, with an illustration of Bazeries' Cylindrical Cryptograph.*

and the starting position – for example, with 'a' on the inner ring opposite 'M' on the outer one.

To encipher a message, it is thought that the letters of the plaintext were spelt out one at a time on the inner disc and the equivalent on the outer ring noted down for transmission. Say, for example, the message concerned contained the word 'message'. After the first 's' had been enciphered, the inner wheel would be turned a full 360 degrees before the second 's' was enciphered. Because of the gearing, the inner ring would go through an entire revolution while the outer ring would go through 26/33rds of a turn; this would result in the second enciphered letter standing seven places further forward. If another 's' was enciphered that would be another seven places ahead. As 33 and 26 have no common factors, the outer ring would go through all 26 letters and seven digits before the letter 's' was enciphered by the same letter again.

Information about Wadsworth's design was not widely disseminated during his lifetime and died with him. His contribution to cryptography has only been recognized posthumously.

Bazeries Cylinder

A century after Jefferson's invention, Étienne Bazeries independently developed his own version of the cipher wheel, called the Bazeries Cylinder. A variant of this, used by the US Army between 1923 and 1942 and known as the M-94, was first proposed by Captain Parker Hitt, author of the *Manual for the Solution of Military Ciphers* published in 1915 at 35 cents. In a memorandum to the director of the Army Signal School dated 19 December 1914, Hitt wrote: 'This device is based, to a certain extent, on the ideas of Commander Bazeries, of the French Army.'

Hitt's variant was called the strip cipher. He simply peeled the jumbled alphabets off the rotors of the Bazeries Cylinder and arranged the resulting strips in an 18 x 8.25cm (7 x 3¼ in) frame. The strips were slid in and out until the first 20 letters of the message were spelt out. Then another line was selected to give the ciphertext. Hitt also made his own cylinder, but preferred his strip method.

Hitt's work came to the attention of Joseph Mauborgne, then heading the Engineering and Research Division of the Signal Corps, who improved the design. The army-issue M-94 consisted of 25 aluminium discs the size of a silver dollar on a spindle 11cm (4¼ in) long. Each disc, apart from one, had the 26 letters of the Roman alphabet scrambled round its circumference, with the letters arranged differently in each case. The seventeenth disc began with the letters 'ARMY OF THE US'. Each disc was stamped with an identifying number and letter; the discs were identified according to the letter following A on each one.

PARKER HITT (1877–1971)

Quitting his civil engineering studies at Purdue University, Parker Hitt joined the US Army during the Spanish–American war of 1898. Commissioned in Cuba, he was posted to the Philippines. He went on to study at the Army Signal School at Fort Leavenworth, Kansas, becoming an instructor there. He and his wife began deciphering intercepted cryptograms from Mexican revolutionaries under Pancho Villa, prior to General John Pershing's punitive raid in 1916. By then, Hitt had published his *Manual for the Solution of Military Ciphers*. When the 4,000 copies of the first edition sold out, a second edition was published, running to 16,000 copies. It became the textbook used to train the cryptanalysts of the American Expeditionary Force. Hitt joined the AEF as Pershing's chief signal officer when it sailed for France in 1917. Aghast at the primitive enciphering machines the army was using, he developed his strip system. While this was developed into the M-94, Hitt's strip system was reintroduced in the 1930s as the M-138-A, and was still in use in World War II when Hitt served again as a corps area signal officer.

Cipher M-94

Disc ID		Letters around the rim
B	1	A B C E I G D J F V U Y M H T Q K Z O L R X S P W N
C	2	A C D E H F I J K T L M O U V Y G Z N P Q X R W S B
D	3	A D K O M J U B G E P H S C Z I N X F Y Q R T V W L
E	4	A E D C B I F G J H L K M R U O Q V P T N W Y X Z S
F	5	A F N Q U K D O P I T J B R H C Y S L W E M Z V X G
G	6	A G P O C I X L U R N D Y Z H W B J S Q F K V M E T
H	7	A H X J E Z B N I K P V R O G S Y D U L C F M Q T W
I	8	A I H P J O B W K C V F Z L Q E R Y N S U M G T D X
J	9	A J D S K Q O I V T Z E F H G Y U N L P M B X W C R
K	10	A K E L B D F J G H O N M T P R Q S V Z U X Y W I C
L	11	A L T M S X V Q P N O H U W D I Z Y C G K R F B E J
M	12	A M N F L H Q G C U J T B Y P Z K X I S R D V E W O
N	13	A N C J I L D H B M K G X U Z T S W Q Y V O R P F E
O	14	A O D W P K J V I U Q H Z C T X B L E G N Y R S M F
P	15	A P B V H I Y K S G U E N T C X O W F Q D R L J Z M
Q	16	A Q J N U B T G I M W Z R V L X C S H D E O K F P Y
R	17	**A R M Y O F T H E U S** Z J X D P C W G Q I B K L N V
S	18	A S D M C N E Q B O Z P L G V J R K Y T F U I W X H
T	19	A T O J Y L F X N G W H V C M I R B S E K U P D Z Q
U	20	A U T R Z X Q L Y I O V B P E S N H J W M D G F C K
V	21	A V N K H R G O X E Y B F S J M U D Q C L Z W T I P
W	22	A W V S F D L I E B H K N R J Q Z G M X P U C O T Y
X	23	A X K W R E V D T U F O Y H M L S I Q N J C P G B Z
Y	24	A Y J P X M V K B Q W U G L O S T E C H N Z F R I D
Z	25	A Z D N B U H Y F W J L V G R C Q M P S O E X T K I

The discs were assembled on the rod in an order which comprised the key. There were 25 factorial possible arrangements – more than 15 septillion possibilities! Even so, it was possible to crack a code enciphered using the M-94. The principle is outlined in Greg Goebel's book *Codes, Ciphers, and Codebreaking*. Goebel uses just ten discs:

```
 1:  ZWAXJGDLUBVIQHKYPNTCRMOSFE
 2:  KPBELNACZDTRXMJQOYHGVSFUWI
 3:  BDMAIZVRNSJUWFHTEQGYXPLOCK
 4:  RPLNDVHGFCUKTEBSXQYIZMJWAO
 5:  IHFRLABEUOTSGJVDKCPMNZQWXY
 6:  AMKGHIWPNYCJBFZDRUSLOQXVET
 7:  GWTHSPYBXIZULVKMRAFDCEONJQ
 8:  NOZUTWDCVRJLXKISEFAPMYGHBQ
 9:  XPLTDSRFHENYVUBMCQWAOIKZGJ
10:  UDNAJFBOWTGVRSCZQKELMXYIHP
```

The discs are loaded on to the spindle according to the designated key 7, 9, 5, 10, 1, 6, 3, 8, 2, 4. To encipher 'retreat now', the sender lines up the letters r, e, t, r, e, a, t, n, o and w, then takes the ciphertext from, say, the sixth letter of the plaintext, picked out here in bold.

The US Army M-94 cipher machine.

```
 7:  R AFDCE O NJQGWTHSPYBXIZULVKM
 9:  E NYVUB M CQWAOIKZGJXPLTDSRFH
 5:  T SGJVD K CPMNZQWXYIHFRLABEUO
10:  R SCZQK E LMXYIHPUDNAJFBOWTGV
 1:  E ZWAXJ G DLUBVIQHKYPNTCRMOSF
 6:  A MKGHI W PNYCJBFZDRUSLOQXVET
 3:  T EQGYX P LOCKBDMAIZVRNSJUWFH
 8:  N OZUTW D CVRJLXKISEFAPMYGHBQ
 2:  O YHGVS F UWIKPBELNACZDTRXMJQ
 4:  W AORPL N DVHGFCUKTEBSXQYIZMJ
```

The ciphertext reads: OMKEGWPDFN

'The enemy had known and deciphered all our codes, even the most difficult and the most secret.'

The Battle of Caporetto in 1917 was one of the most decisive exchanges of World War I. An Austro-Hungarian and German surprise attack ended in disaster for the Italian Army. The post-war commission of enquiry, quoted above, fixed the blame for Italy's defeat on intercepted wireless transmissions.

JOSEPH MAUBORGNE
(1881–1971)

After graduating from the Army Signal School at Fort Leavenworth, Kansas, in 1910, Joseph Mauborgne dedicated his career to improving US military cryptography. He was the first to solve the Playfair cipher, used by the British as their field cipher, publishing his solution in *An Advanced Problem in Cryptography and Its Solution* in 1914. This was the first cryptological pamphlet published by the US government.

Mauborge continued his career in the army, rising to become Chief of Signals. He was also a widely exhibited artist, an internationally recognized violin-maker and a renowned marksman.

CODE TALKING

The American armed forces started using complex Native American languages as military code during World War I. Towards the end of the war, a group of Choctaw Indians from Oklahoma pioneered the use of Native American languages as military code. The government of the Choctaw Nation maintains that the men were the first native code talkers ever to serve in the US military. An American officer, Colonel A. W. Bloor, was serving alongside a number of American Indians in the 142nd Infantry in France. Overhearing two Choctaw Indians speaking to each another, he realized he could not understand them. He also saw that if he could not understand them, the same would be true for the Germans, no matter how good their English skills. Native Americans were already serving as messengers and runners between units. By placing Choctaws in each company, the US military could transmit messages regardless of whether the radio was overheard or the telephone lines tapped.

HERBERT O. YARDLEY (1889–1958)

Trained as a railroad telegrapher by his father, Herbert Yardley moved from Indiana to Washington, D.C. in 1913, where he worked for the State Department. Self-taught in cryptanalysis, he found he could break the department's codes and ciphers. When the US declared war on Germany in April 1917, Yardley joined the US Army Signal Corps where he set up the Cipher Bureau of the Military Intelligence Division, MI-8. According to Yardley, over the following 18 months the bureau broke 578 codes and ciphers and decrypted 10,735 messages, including the one that condemned German spy Lothar Witzke.

In August 1918, Yardley travelled to Europe to learn from the British and the French. After the war he convinced the State Department that it needed a cryptology department and, detached from the military, the Cipher Bureau moved to New York City. Japan was seen as being belligerent at the time and Yardley and his staff succeeded in breaking its codes and reading its diplomatic traffic during the crucial Washington Naval Conference of 1921–2, which had been called to limit the naval arms race. But when President Herbert

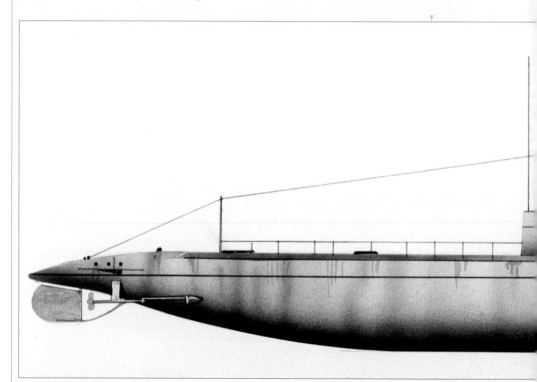

The Washington Naval Conference in 1921-2 limited the participants' submarine fleets, as well as their battleships, while Yardley and his Cipher Bureau listened in on friend and foe alike.

Hoover appointed Henry L. Stimson secretary of state in 1929, he closed the Cipher Bureau on the grounds that 'gentlemen do not read each other's mail'.

Following the Wall Street Crash, Yardley saved his family from penury by writing *The American Black Chamber*. 'The Black Chamber,' he wrote, 'bolted, hidden, guarded, sees all, hears all. Though the blinds are drawn and the windows heavily curtained, its far seeking eyes penetrate the secret conference chambers at Washington, Tokyo, London, Paris, Geneva, Rome. Its sensitive ears catch the faintest whisperings in the foreign capitals of the world.' The book became an international bestseller. The US government's reaction was to amend the Espionage Act, prohibiting the disclosure of foreign codes or anything sent in code. Consequently, Yardley's second book, *Japanese Diplomatic Codes 1921–22*, was impounded.

Yardley wrote three spy novels and a book about the mathematics of poker. During World War II, he carried out cryptographic work for Canada and China. His book describing his experiences in China, *The Chinese Black Chamber*, was declassified and published in 1983.

The weakness of this method of encipherment is that the offset from the plaintext to the ciphertext is the same for each disc. As can be seen, all the letters in the plaintext line up to make the message legible, and all the letters in the ciphertext also line up.

To break the code, you need a 'crib' – this is a stock phrase likely to crop up frequently in coded communications. A crib the Allies used to good effect when cracking German codes in World War II was 'Heil Hitler', which loyal Nazis would often use to begin or end messages. It has, conveniently, ten letters.

So, if a message suspected of ending with 'Heil Hitler' concluded with the ciphertext AZNCZEAPBH, it would be reasonable to begin attempts to break it by assuming that h=A, e=Z, i=N, l=C, h=Z, i=E, t=A, l=P, e=B and r=H.

In our current example, disc one of Goebel's cipher reads as follows:

1:    ZWAXJGDLUBVIQHKYPNTCRMOSFE

The offset between 'h' and 'A' is 15, counting the letters from left to right and going back to the beginning when you get to the end. Taking the second letters, 'e' and 'Z', we get an offset of one, as E is at the end and Z is at the beginning. The procedure is continued with the first disc for each of the letter pairs. Then the same is done for the other nine discs and a table is drawn up:

H:A	E:Z	I:N	L:C	H:Z	I:E	T:A	L:P	E:B	R:H
1: 15	1	6	12	13	14	10	9	10	19
2: 14	5	6	3	16	4	22	23	25	7

3: 15	15	4	2	17	12	14	25	10	7
4: 18	7	10	7	14	20	12	25	1	6
5: 4	14	20	13	20	7	21	14	25	24
6: 22	16	3	17	10	19	1	14	14	14
7: 14	15	14	8	7	12	15	19	12	13
8: 21	12	12	22	5	2	14	8	8	14
9: 11	14	15	14	15	14	16	25	5	2
10: 5	23	5	21	17	21	20	6	14	12

It is evident that every line carries the number 14. Indeed, it is the only number that occurs in all ten lines, so it is the offset between the crib in plaintext and the ciphertext. Removing the other numbers, it can be seen clearly:

H:A	E:Z	I:N	L:C	H:Z	I:E	T:A	L:P	E:B	R:H
1: -	-	-	-	-	14	-	-	-	-
2: 14	-	-	-	-	-	-	-	-	-
3: -	-	-	-	-	-	14	-	-	-
4: -	-	-	-	14	-	-	-	-	-
5: -	14	-	-	-	-	-	14	-	-
6: -	-	-	-	-	-	-	14	14	14
7: 14	-	14	-	-	-	-	-	-	-
8: -	-	-	-	-	-	14	-	-	14
9: -	14	-	14	-	14	-	-	-	-
10: -	-	-	-	-	-	-	-	14	-

It is then a matter of rearranging the lines to create a diagonal:

H:A	E:Z	I:N	L:C	H:Z	I:E	T:A	L:P	E:B	R:H
2: 14	-	-	-	-	-	-	-	-	-
5: -	14	-	-	-	-	-	14	-	-
7: 14	-	14	-	-	-	-	-	-	-
9: -	14	-	14	-	14	-	-	-	-
4: -	-	-	-	14	-	-	-	-	-
1: -	-	-	-	-	14	-	-	-	-
3: -	-	-	-	-	-	14	-	-	-
6: -	-	-	-	-	-	-	14	14	14

86

```
10:  -   -   -   -   -   -   - 14  -
 8:  -   -   -   -   - 14   -   - 14
```

This reflects the order of the rotors, giving the key: 2, 5, 7, 9, 4, 1, 3, 6, 10, 8.

If there were any other arrangement which gave that smooth diagonal, it would be easy to test it and find out which one works. Clearly, with the M-94, there was unlikely to be a crib that ran across all 25 rotors. However, if the crib was just five or six letters long, it would be possible to build up a table of offsets for each possible pair, greatly reducing the possibilities. Military communications often conform to a fairly standard format. The world 'division', or the name of a particular general, is likely to come up frequently.

An unbreakable key

After helping to design the M-94, Mauborgne developed an unbreakable key. He did this while testing a system of automatic encipherment devised by AT&T engineer Gilbert Vernam in 1918. It used punched paper tape with letters encoded on it using the Baudot code, a form of what we would recognize as binary. A tape carrying the plaintext was passed through the encoding machine at the same time as a second tape carrying the key. It would then be encoded on a third tape, using what we now recognize as an XOR gate:

```
  HOLE    +   HOLE     = NO-HOLE
  HOLE    + NO-HOLE    =  HOLE
NO-HOLE   +   HOLE     =  HOLE
NO-HOLE   + NO-HOLE    = NO-HOLE
```

Or in binary:

$$0 + 0 = 0$$
$$1 + 0 = 1$$
$$0 + 1 = 1$$
$$1 + 1 = 0$$

To decipher the encrypted message, it just has to be run through the machine again using the same key. The result is the message in plaintext. However, Mauborgne recognized that the weakness of the Vernam system was that the key was on a loop. He realized that the solution would be to have an endless key tape. While this was not practical, the same result could be achieved by having a key the same length as the message itself, making it the mechanical equivalent of using a one-time pad. Even if you had the ciphertext and the plaintext, and had worked out the key, it would be of no good to you, as the chances of the same key occurring again, with a message of any length, were vanishingly small.

Wheatstone's cipher

Although Wheatstone's earlier contribution to cryptography has been misattributed to Lord Playfair, he struck back in 1867, displaying his 'Cryptograph' at the

> 'Let the key for the foregoing table be a line of poetry or the name of some memorable person or place, which cannot easily be forgotten.'
>
> Admiral Sir Francis Beaufort, instructions to enciphering cards, 1857

BAUDOT CODE

Devised in 1874 by French engineer Jean-Maurice-Émile Baudot, the Baudot code had an advantage over Morse code as it comprised five-unit combinations of current-on or current-off signals of equal duration. This made it more suitable for use with teleprinters.

A	11000
B	10011
C	01110
D	10010
E	10000
F	10110
G	01011
H	00101
I	01100
J	11010
K	11110
L	01001
M	00111
N	00110
O	01101
Q	11101
R	01010
S	10100
U	11100
V	01111
W	11001
X	10111
Y	10101
Z	10001

As there are 32 combinations of five binary digits, the remaining six are used as machine controls:

Paragraph break	01000
Carriage return	00010
Number/letter shift	11111
Letter/number shift	11011
Idle	00100
Blank space	00000

The Baudot telegraph system eventually replaced hand-keyed Morse code.

Exposition Universelle in Paris. It was similar to Wadsworth's machine (see page 79), with 26 letters on the inner ring and 26 letters plus one space (27 elements in all) on the outer ring, known as the 'despatch'. Over them swung two clock-like hands, connected by gears in the ratio of 26:27. The long hand pointed to the letters on the outer ring while the little hand picked out letters on the inner ring.

Wheatstone's instructions for enciphering read: 'At the commencement the long hand must correspond to the blank of the outer circle and the short hand be directly under it. The long hand must be brought successively to the letters of the despatch, and the letters indicated on the inner circle by the short hand must be written down. At the termination of each word the long hand must be brought to the blank, and the letter indicated by the short hand also written down. By this arrangement, the cipher is continuous, no intimation being given of the separation of the words. Whenever a double letter occurs, some unused letter (as, for instance, q) must always be substituted for the repeated letter; or the latter may be omitted.'

Again, the gearing meant that when the long hand had completed one revolution the little hand had already advanced one cell into its second revolution. As the alphabets were laid out in the regular order, double letters in the plaintext would be rendered as adjacent letters in reverse order in the ciphertext, such as BA and DC. This was a weakness, and is why Wheatstone recommended substituting a 'q'.

To decipher the message, the long hand was turned until the short hand pointed to the letters of the ciphertext on the inner circle; then the plaintext, with its original spaces, could be read from the outer ring.

For additional secrecy, the 26 letters could be inscribed on 26 small pieces of card and slotted into place in the inner circle, then removed when the cryptograph was not in use. Colonel Laussedat who headed a French commission into examining exhibits for their military uses proclaimed that the Wheatstone Cryptograph 'assures the most absolute secrecy'. However, just four years later, *Macmillan's Magazine* printed a solution based on the probability of a large number of sentences beginning with the word 'the'.

CHARLES WHEATSTONE (1802–75)

Wheatstone was apprenticed at the age of 14 to an uncle, a musical instrument maker. He took over the business when his uncle died in 1823, publishing that same year in *Annals of Philosophy* details of his experiments with sound. Ten years later he was demonstrating further experiments to the Royal Society. Wheatstone invented the stereoscope and demonstrated that electric sparks from different metals produced differing spectrums. He also invented a clock that could tell the time from the sun, even when it was cloudy.

With his collaborator William Fothergill Cooke, Wheatstone was the first to make the telegraph available for public transmission and developed the type-printing telegraph in 1841. He was also a pioneer in submarine telegraphy. His capacity to decipher hieroglyphs led him to cryptology.

THE CAPTURE OF LOTHAR WITZKE

Born in Posen in 1895, Lothar Witzke was a lieutenant in the Imperial German Navy when his ship SMS *Dresden* was sunk by the Royal Navy during World War I. Witzke was interned with the rest of the crew in Valparaiso, Chile. Escaping to the USA, he became a saboteur. He was thought to be behind the Black Tom explosion on 30 July 1916, where a thousand tons of munitions awaiting shipment to the Allies were blown up in New York harbour. In February 1918, Witzke was arrested on the Mexican border; he was using the name Pablo Waberski and purporting to be a Russian-American. He had a document with him containing 424 letters of ciphertext. It was sent to MI-8, where Dr John M. Manly, professor of English literature and philology at the University of Chicago, along with his assistant Edith Rickert, set about decoding it. After three days, they reasoned that it was a 12-step transposition code which read:

> *'The bearer of this is a subject of the Empire who travels as a Russian under the name Pablo Waberski. He is a German secret agent. Please furnish him on request protection and assistance; also advance him on demand up to 1,000 pesos of Mexican gold and send his code telegrams to this embassy as consular despatches.'*

Manly read this out in the courtroom at Fort Sam Houston in San Antonio, where Witzke was standing trial for espionage. Witzke was convicted and sentenced to death, but the sentence was commuted to life imprisonment. He was released in 1923 and sent back to Germany, where he was awarded the Iron Cross.

SMS *Dresden.*

CHAPTER 7

MAKING ENIGMA

'By 1945 the Nazis had deployed over 100,000 of these electronic lookalike typewriters, which beneath their innocuous appearance housed an extremely sophisticated cipher system.'

Tessa Dunlop,
The Bletchley Girls, 2015

Realizing that the codes they used in World War I had been broken easily by the Allies, the German military turned to the Enigma machine. Developed by electrical engineer Arthur Scherbius, it used a system of wired rotors that advanced as each letter was encrypted.

A rotor from an Enigma machine, showing the complex wiring. Although mathematically any message encoded on it was theoretically unbreakable, the German authorities showed little interest in Enigma – at first.

The Scherbius machine

In Germany, long before the end of World War I, electrical engineer Arthur Scherbius (see box) realized that the old paper-and-pencil method of enciphering secret messages was hopelessly out of date in the era of mechanized warfare. On 23 February 1918, he applied for a patent on a cipher machine that used rotating wired wheels.

During the Spring Offensive of that year, Scherbius wrote to the Imperial German Navy about it, enclosing details of the patent. His machine, he said, 'would avoid any repetition of a sequence of letters when the same letter is struck millions of times'. What was more: 'The solution of a telegram is also impossible if a machine falls into unauthorized hands, since it requires a prearranged key system.'

The rotor

Enciphering on a Scherbius machine depended on a simple rotor. This was a disc with, usually, 26 contacts on either side corresponding to the letters of the alphabet. The discs were wired in such a way that the contact corresponding to the letter 'A' on the input side was connected to Y, say, on the output side.

The plaintext message was fed into a keyboard which sent a small electric current to an input plate that made contact with one side of the rotor. The other side of the rotor made contact with an output plate that passed the current to a bulb, which illuminated a letter on a glass screen.

Had the rotor not moved, a simple monoalphabetic substitution cipher would have been given by the wiring in the wheel. As it was, the stroke of the typewriter key

turned the rotor forward one letter, or 1/26th of a revolution. The connections within the rotor would then be different and a different letter would be illuminated. If the letter 'l' was pressed twice in succession, the first time it might come out as a P, the second time as an E. If you pressed the same key 26 times, you would get back to where you started.

However, if another rotor was added that moved forward 1/26th of a turn for each full rotation of the first, the machine would go through 26 x 26 (or 676) cycles before it got back to the beginning again. A third rotor would give 17,576 cycles. Four rotors would give 456,976 cycles, and five 11,881,376.

The three-rotor Enigma cipher machine.

To decipher the code, the recipient needed to know the initial position of each rotor. This was known as the 'key'. With 26 positions for each rotor, the key possibilities similarly become astronomical. Scherbius explained:

> 'The key variation is so great that, without knowledge of the key, even with an available plaintext and ciphertext and with the possession of a machine, the key cannot be found, since it is impossible to run through six billion (seven rotors) or a hundred trillion (thirteen rotors) keys. If the examination of each telegram takes half-a-minute in a twenty-four-hour workday, this would require 5.8 years with the simultaneous employment of a hundred machines of seven rotors and 14.5 years for a thousand machines of eight rotors.... It would only make sense to search for a key in this way when it is known that unknown cryptograms have the same key, and when the same key is maintained for a long time.'

Scherbius was offering a ten-rotor machine for 4,000 to 5,000 marks ($560 to $720, or $9,000 to $11,500 in today's prices). Delivery was promised in eight weeks. But even though the German Navy acknowledged the virtues of the machine, with the fleet confined to port after the Battle of Jutland, naval cipher traffic did not warrant the investment.

The navy directed Scherbius to the Foreign Ministry, but they were not interested either. They believed the British story about the plaintext of the Zimmermann telegram being stolen in Mexico City and thought their codes were secure. Undaunted, Scherbius sought commercial outlets for his invention.

ARTHUR SCHERBIUS (1878–1929)

Arthur Scherbius was born in Frankfurt am Main, Germany, and studied electricity at technical college in Munich, graduating in 1903. The following year he was awarded a doctorate in engineering for his dissertation *Proposal for the Construction of an Indirect Water Turbine Governor*. He worked for major electrical companies in Germany and Switzerland, inventing (among other things) a high-voltage electric motor designed to handle sudden changes of stress. His first electrical enciphering machine turned numbers into pronounceable words, which were charged at a lower rate by the telegraph companies. This used multiple cross-wired switchboards, which may have formed the basis for the wiring in the rotors of the Enigma machine. In 1918, Scherbius founded the firm Scherbius & Ritter with certified engineer E. Richard Ritter and began marketing Enigma machines, mainly to banks. In the 1920s, the military finally took an interest, but orders were low. Then, in 1929, Scherbius was killed when a horse-drawn wagon he was driving smashed into a wall. Nevertheless, the company he had founded continued to produce Enigma machines.

Named the Enigma, the machine was exhibited at the congress of the International Postal Union in 1923. A version that printed out the message was 38cm (15in) high and weighed more than 45kg (100lb). Soon there was a version that was only 11cm (4½in) high and weighed just 7kg (15lb). It had four rotors with toothed thumbwheels poking through the lid to make the initial settings. There were three rows of typewriter keys to input the plaintext, and three lines of letters in circular windows above, with bulbs behind them to read out the ciphertext one letter at a time.

Refinements followed quickly: the rotors were made detachable, so the order could be switched round. The fourth rotor was changed to a 'reflector' that did not move and had contacts on one side only, connected to each other in pairs. Its effect was to send the current back through the three movable rotors down a different path. The advantage of this was that the machine could encipher and decipher without changing configuration. The disadvantage was that if, for example, a plaintext 'a' gave the ciphertext Z, a plaintext 'z' became ciphertext A. It also meant that no letter could be enciphered as itself. This was a flaw which could be exploited.

John Arbuthnot Fisher, painted by Sir Hubert von Herkomer.

Elucidation

The Enigma machine was getting good press, but few were being sold. Meanwhile, the victorious Allies of World War I were publishing their memoirs. As early as 1919, former First Sea Lord Baron John Fisher mentioned in his *Memories* that the 'elucidation' of the enemy's ciphers was one of the crowing glories of the Admiralty, boasting: 'In my time, they never failed once in that elucidation.'

In his bestselling *The World Crisis* in 1923, Winston Churchill mentioned the codebooks taken from the *Magdeburg* and how German radio messages had been intercepted and deciphered by the British.

The Imperial German Navy quickly reconsidered. By 1925, Scherbius and Ritter's new company, the Cipher Machine Stock Corporation, was supplying it with Enigma machines. These versions had an alphabetical keyboard, instead of one with the standard German typewriter layout. They also had 29 contacts on each wheel. This was because the various naval codebooks, which were used to encode messages before they were enciphered, included words with the umlauted letters ä, ö and ü. And while the machine only used three rotors, it was supplied with five, adding more possibilities to the encipherment. Officers alone were allowed to set the rotor positions. To avoid repetition, these formulations were listed in a booklet. Whichever formulation was being used was sent as a group of letters, which was then enciphered.

At this point, the German Army became interested, but required some modifications. They wanted a keyboard with the standard German layout, with QWERTZUIO appearing on the top row of keys. (The top line of the standard Anglo-American keyboard reads QWERTYUIOP, but in Germany P and Y appeared on the bottom row of keys.)

The army Enigma machine went into service in July 1928. By then its price had dropped to 600 Reichsmarks. But commercial sales remained slow and only a few hundred units were sold to the military,

> *'It was generally believed that no civilized nation that had once been through the traumatic experience of having its ciphers read would ever allow it to happen again.'*
> Josh Cooper, chief cryptographer, GCCS

whose size and activities were now limited by the Versailles Treaty. The army dispensed with codebooks and booklets containing standard settings, and the operator would make up a new key for each message.

The plugboard

The German Army experimented briefly with an eight-rotor machine, but opted instead for another innovation – the fitting of a plugboard with 26 sockets between the keyboard and the first rotor. Short cables with jack plugs on either end connected pairs. If nothing was plugged into the socket equivalent to A, the signal was passed on as an A. But if A was connected to the socket equivalent to T, then a T was sent on, while a T was sent as an A. This alone could produce up to 200 million million possibilities. To keep the operation from becoming too complicated, the army only connected six pairs of letters, giving an extra layer of encipherment to 12 letters. The rest were enciphered by the rotors alone.

In 1930, the German Navy agreed to take the army machine with its plugboard, but insisted on extra rotors. The standard army model had three rotors – I, II and III. The navy used those only when communicating with the army. Rotors IV and V were held in reserve, while VI and VII were used for communication within the navy itself.

Rotors I to V turned the rotor to the left only one letter for each revolution it made, but rotors VI and VII had a second notch cut – next to the H and the U – which turned the rotor to the left an extra space.

In 1935, Hitler began tearing up the Versailles Treaty and started a massive expansion of the German armed forces. Soon there was a huge demand for Enigma machines from all branches of the military and also from the security forces. Even the police and the railways took them.

Standardized procedures

The spread of the Enigma cryptographic system meant a tightening of security and a standardization of procedures. Before enciphering a message, the operator had to move the rotors to an agreed starting position. With three rotors, there were 17,576 possible starting positions. The initial settings were taken from a codebook that listed the key for each day.

Once the rotors were set, the operator keyed in the message letter by letter, noting down which letters were illuminated in the display. Once the whole message had been enciphered, this ciphertext was handed on to the wireless operator who transmitted it in Morse code.

The wireless operator receiving the message wrote down the letters of the ciphertext and handed them on to the operator manning the Enigma machine.

THE COMPETITION

Enigma was not the only machine to use wired rotors to encrypt. The Swedish textile engineer Arvid Gerhard Damm applied for a patent in Stockholm in October 1919 three days after Hugo Koch had done so in the Netherlands. Koch's machine was never made and his patent was sold to Scherbius.

Immediately before World War I, Damm and Huddersfield cloth-maker George Lorimer Craig had filed three patent applications for cipher machines at the German patent office. With Captain Olof Gyldén, commander of the Royal Naval School in Stockholm, Damm set up Aktiebolaget Cryptograph, or Cryptograph, Inc. They developed a number of machines. The Mecano-Cryptographer Model A-1 printed the plaintext results, giving it an advantage over Enigma. However, it proved unreliable in tests in 1925.

Boris Hagelin joined the company and simplified the machine, making it a direct rival to the Enigma and selling a large number to the Swedish Army. When Damm died in 1927, Hagelin took over. The French general staff asked him to build a cipher machine that would fit in a pocket. He produced a model just 6 x 4½ x 2in and the French ordered 5,000 in 1935.

Hagelin was already in touch with the US authorities when war broke out in Europe in 1939. With the invasion of Norway, Hagelin and his wife escaped across Europe carrying blueprints and dismantled prototypes. Sailing from Genoa, they reached North America safely. The US Army liked what they saw. More than 140,000 of his machines were produced by Smith Corona Typewriters, making Hagelin a millionaire.

This was also set up with that day's rotor settings. The ciphertext was then keyed in a letter at a time and the letters illuminated on the display would produce the plaintext.

Had the Germans been using a simple three-rotor machine, it would have been possible, theoretically, to crack any code within a day. But once the three rotors could be removed and replaced in any order, it increased the possibilities six-fold to 105,456. But the plugboard alone, swapping six pairs of letters out of 26, renders another 100,391,791,500 possibilities. Altogether there are somewhere in the region of 10,000,000,000,000,000 possible permutations of the rotor and plugboard settings. To check those at one a minute would take longer than the age of the universe. This arrangement, Scherbius considered, produced a cipher that was unbreakable.

The German military bought over 30,000 Enigma machines, giving their communications an unparalleled level of security. Having learned the painful lessons of World War I, the Nazis believed that Enigma would play a vital part in their ultimate victory in World War II. Not for the first time, the belief that their codes were unbreakable proved to be an Achilles' heel and contributed mightily to Germany's downfall.

German soldiers returning after World War I – following its defeat, Germany would become determined not to fall foul of Allied codebreakers again.

CHAPTER 8

BREAKING ENIGMA

'It is often forgotten, however, that the Polish cryptanalysis improved the morale as well as the working methods of British codebreakers.'

Professor Christopher Andrew,
Polish-British Historical Committee,
quoted in *Living with the Enigma Secret*

British codebreakers believed Enigma was unbreakable, but were not too concerned because the Versailles Treaty had curtailed Germany's military forces. The real menace was the new Communist government in Russia, preaching world revolution. Poland, however, felt threatened from both east and west, and employed a trio of mathematicians to spot flaws in Enigma.

The message would first be encrypted using the Enigma machine to the left. The result would then be handed to the radio operator who would transmit it in Morse code.

Polish intelligence

In 1929, the USA's Cipher Bureau had closed down. France had cut its army cryptanalysts back to just eight staff. Room 40 had merged with British Army intelligence unit M11b to form the Government Code and Cypher School. Now Poland found itself on the front line of cryptography.

Lying between Germany and Russia, Poland had a troubled history. In the 18th century, its territory was carved up among Prussia, Russia and Austria, until Poland as a separate entity ceased to exist. When the Polish state re-emerged in 1918, it was immediately threatened by the Soviet Union, freshly created from the old Russian empire.

However, decrypts supplied by the Polish Cipher Bureau set up by Jan Kowalewski allowed the fledgling Polish Army to halt the Soviets at the gates of Warsaw and drive them back.

Poland then came under threat from the east. The Versailles Treaty, which had re-established Polish independence, gave Poland access to the Baltic Sea along what became known as the 'Polish corridor'. This separated East Prussia from the rest of Germany, and had made the port of Danzig, or Gdansk, a free city under the sovereignty of the League of Nations (though administered by Poland). This led to a great deal of German resentment, which was played upon by Adolf Hitler during the Nazis' rise to power. Poland's refusal to hand over Gdansk was Hitler's excuse for invading the country in 1939.

When the fledgling Soviet Red Army tried to invade the newly independent Poland, it was thwarted by the Polish Cipher Bureau.

JAN KOWALEWSKI (1892–1965)

After studying chemistry at the University of Liège, Jan Kowalewski returned to Poland in 1913, where he was conscripted into the Russian Army to fight in World War I. He served in the Engineering and Signal Corps until Russian capitulation in 1917, then became chief of intelligence of the Polish 4th Rifle Division. In 1919, he was serving on the Polish general staff when a friend asked him to take over his duties while he went on leave to get married. The friend's work involved translating and evaluating intercepted telegrams. One day, a Russia intercept in code landed on his desk. Intrigued he set about cracking it. The message concerned the movement of White Russian forces fighting the Reds in the Russian civil war.

Having discovered intelligence of some importance to the Poles, who were then involved in a war with Ukraine, he was transferred to the radio-intelligence department in Warsaw. There he recruited mathematicians to crack more Russian codes and was award the Silver Cross of the Virtuti Militari, Poland's highest military decoration, for his part in Poland's victory in the Polish–Soviet war.

In 1923, he went to Tokyo to run a course in radio intelligence for Japanese officers. He then studied at the École Supérieure de Guerre in Paris. Serving as military attaché in Moscow, he was expelled from Russia in 1929.

In 1939, when the invasion of Poland by Nazi Germany triggered World War II, Kowalewski escaped through Romania to France where he joined the Polish Army in exile. With the fall of France in 1940, he fled to Portugal, where he co-ordinated intelligence and resistance work. Though his activities proved invaluable to the British, he irritated their Soviet allies, who demanded his withdrawal. He was transferred to the Polish Operations Bureau in London, which was then preparing for D-Day. After the war, he remained in exile in England, where he took an interest in some historical cryptanalysis, breaking the codes used by Polish nationalist Romuald Traugutt in the January Uprising of 1864.

In 1920, Dmitry Moor designed a striking poster, 'Bud' na strazhe!' ('Be on Guard!') which featured a drawing of Trotsky, Soviet minister of war, standing, larger than life, on Russian territory with minuscule enemies around him.

Reading German codes

Germany's growing hostility led Poland to sign a treaty with France. The Polish Cipher Bureau now turned its attention to reading German intercepts. In 1926, they noticed that German naval cryptograms had changed. Two years later, German Army codes also became unreadable. The bureau then discovered that this was because the messages were being encrypted mechanically, so they bought an Enigma machine. But they found that there were not enough messages encrypted with any one key for them to crack the code by superimposition. This is the method (described on page 48) of discovering the key length, then breaking down the polyalphabetic cipher into a series of monoalphabetic ciphers that can be cracked by frequency analysis. However, to do this, the codebreakers needed a large amount of traffic encoded using the same key.

'I don't know what would have happened if dad had stayed in Poland. During the war various gentlemen would turn up at our house asking about father. Mum always gave the same answer, that she didn't know where he was or what he was up to.'

Janina Sylwestrzak, daughter of Marian Rejewski

students cryptograms to solve. Among the recruits they attracted were Marian Rejewski (see box), Henryk Zygalski and Jerzy Rózycki. They set to work on the Germany Navy intercepts. First they noticed that many code groups began with the letter Y. They reasoned that these were

Mathematicians

It was clear the old, intuitive method that classical scholars and linguists had used for cracking codes was no longer effective – they needed mathematicians. The Cipher Bureau (*Biuro Szyfrów*), now designated BS-4, went head-hunting in Poznán. This has been in the German part of Poland during the partition, so the students there had been schooled in German.

BS-4 analysts started classes in cryptology, giving

The Second Polish Republic, 1921-39, showing the Polish corridor between the main body of Germany and German East Prussia, both shown in orange.

MARIAN REJEWSKI (1905–80)

In 1929, mathematics student Marian Rejewski attended a course on cryptography in Poznán. Two years later he joined the Biuro Szyfrów, where fellow students Henryk Zygalski and Jerzy Rózycki were already employed. Together they broke a four-letter code used by the German Navy. He then moved on to the Enigma code. Spotting cycles in the indicator, or six-letter message key at the beginning of each intercept, he cracked the Enigma and deduced the wiring of the rotors. He also designed the *bomba*, which mechanically revealed the day-keys the Germans were using. Details were handed over to the British and French.

When the Germans invaded Poland, the three Polish cryptologists escaped through Romania to France, where they continued work on Enigma. From there, they communicated with Bletchley Park where Alan Turing (see page 119) was further developing their pioneering work. The cryptologists in France and Britain communicated using Polish replica Enigma machines, signing off with an ironic 'Heil Hitler'. After the fall of France, the Poles continued to work in North Africa and in Vichy France. Rózycki was killed when the French passenger ship on which he was returning from Algeria was sunk.

questions. Interrogative speech in German, as in English, begins with: *wer, was, wo, wann* (who, what, where, when).

Then the analysts noticed that a six-group message beginning with YPOY was answered with a four-group message. This, they assumed, was a number – a year perhaps? The solution to the six-group question was: *Wann wurde Friedrick der Grosse geborn?* – 'When was Frederick the Great Born?' The four-digit answer was: 1712.

The luck of the French

The French were also trying to break Enigma, but making no headway. Then they got lucky. In 1931, Gustave Bertrand, Head of Section D (*Décrytement et Interceptions*) of the intelligence service, received a letter from Prague offering to sell important German documents. A French agent codenamed REX was sent to meet the letter's author, Hans-Thilo Schmidt, in Belgium. Schmidt was the younger brother of the former head of the

'There is no question that Knox grasped everything very quickly, almost quick as lightning. It was evident that the British really had been working on Enigma. So they didn't require many explanations.'

Marian Rejewski's account of meeting British cryptographer Dilly Knox in Paris, 1939

German Army Cipher Centre (*Chiffrierstelle*) who had authorized the use of the Enigma machine. Hans-Thilo Schmidt also worked there after the soap factory he owned went bust during the hyperinflation and economic collapse of post-war Germany. Although a member of the Nazi Party, Schmidt had become disaffected.

REX concluded that the documents Schmidt had were genuine, and set up a meeting with Bertrand. Among the documents Schmidt was selling was the instruction manual for the Enigma machine. Bertrand paid 10,000 marks for it, but back in Paris found that the manual was of little use. It did not give details of the rotor wiring or the vital keys.

Although the information gleaned from Hans-Thilo Schmidt's documents was of no help to the French or British, it provided vital details to the Polish codebreakers, who were already far ahead of their allies in the cryptanalysis of Enigma. They had known nothing of the plugboard, as the commercial machine did not have one. They immediately set about building replicas. Armed with these, Rejewski made a renewed attack on Enigma. Meanwhile, in meetings throughout 1931 and 1932, Schmidt provided Bertrand and REX with some of the day keys.

THE FRENCH CONNECTION

Gustave Bertrand played a vital if unwitting part in the breaking of Enigma, passing on information he thought was of little value, but which proved vital to the Poles. He only learned that they had cracked Enigma at the meeting between the French, British and Poles near Warsaw in July 1939.

After the invasion of France, Bertrand and his agents were in danger. REX, aka Rodolphe Lemoine (though born Rudolf Stahlmann in Berlin), was arrested by the Gestapo. Although he refused to work as a double agent for the Germans, saying that they had held him too long to retain any credibility with the French, he did betray Hans-Thilo Schmidt, who was also arrested. Schmidt

died in custody, possibly by taking cyanide pills smuggled to him. Stahlmann knew nothing of the Polish cracking of Enigma. He was taken to Berlin. At the end of the war, he was captured and interrogated by the French, and died in 1946.

Bertrand was also arrested by the Gestapo. Suspecting he was working for the British, they tried to get him to become a double agent. Pretending to agree, he was released. He then went into hiding, eventually making his way to England. Returning to France after the war, he wrote *Enigma ou la plus grande énigme de la guerre 1939–1945* (*Enigma, or the Greatest Enigma of the War of 1939–1945*), the first book to reveal the breaking of the Enigma code.

At Bletchley Park, Alan Turing took Marian Rejewski's bomba *and improved it, then set up banks of them to break the German Navy's Enigma code.*

Spotting a weakness

Rejewski had already noted that messages began with a distinctive six-letter code group. From Schmidt's documents, he learned that to set up the Enigma machine, the operator first plugged in the plugboard according to the key list. Then the rotors were inserted in the order specified for that quarter of the year. Next the alphabet rings were set so that the spring-driven stud which tripped the turn of the next rotor was adjacent to the letter given in the key list for that day. The rotors were turned until the key letters for that day showed in the windows in the machine covers. The operator then thought up a three-letter code unique for the message, for example, PWL, and enciphered it twice (PWLPWL). The resulting code – OHVQNS, say – would be transmitted. The operator then turned the rotors so that the letters PWL showed in the windows and began enciphering the message itself.

The recipient would already have gone through the small process of setting up the Enigma machine. When he received the first six letters of the message and deciphered them, he would get PWLPWL (the message key was sent twice so the recipient could be sure that it was not garbled). He would then set the rotors to show PWL, so deciphering of the body of the message could begin.

Although Rejewski didn't know the day key, the message key or the plugboard settings of the intercepts he was receiving, he knew there was a relationship between the first and fourth letters of the message, as well as the second and fifth, and the third and sixth. In each case, they were the encryption of the same letter and the relationship between them reflected the starting positions of the rotors.

Rejewski began writing tables of the relationships between the letters and found that, if he had enough intercepts on one day, he could build up a complete set of these relationships. The first letter A, for example, might be related to the fourth letter, P. The first letter P might then be related to the fourth letter F. Then the first letter F was related to the fourth letter A, taking the chain back to the beginning again. He discovered that there were chains like this for all the letters that appeared in the first and fourth, second and fifth, and third and sixth positions.

These changed every day: sometimes there were a few long chains with numerous links; other times there were lots of short chains with few links. The important thing was that the number of chains and links depended only on the order of the rotors and the day key, not the plugboard settings. The plugboard only swapped one letter for another and did not change the length of the chain. Rejewski had cut the number of possibilities

A Wehrmacht Enigma key sheet – 'Special Machine key BGS'.

down by a factor of 100,391,791,500, from 10,000,000,000,000,000 to 105,456, which was the number of the initial rotor configurations (17,576, multiplied by the number of rotor arrangements (6)).

Cataloguing the chains

Rejewski's team started combing through each of the 105,456 rotor settings and cataloguing the chain lengths for each one. This took a year to complete. Once it was done, it would take a day's intercepts to work out the chain lengths, which were like a fingerprint. Rejewski could then go to the catalogue and look up which rotor settings gave that set of chain lengths. This gave him the day key.

Rejewski still did not know the plugboard settings, so when he ran the intercept through his replica Enigma machine it delivered rubbish. But occasionally it rendered clues. If LEIHLITHER appeared, it was clear that this read HEILHITLER and the plugboard had connected the H and L, swapping them

The Enigma's plugboard, or Steckerbrett, *was added to the front of the machine, below the input keys.*

number of possible arrangements from six to 60. Rejewski was faced with building ten times as many *bombas*. On top of that, the number of plugboard cables was increased from six to ten, and Schmidt had broken off contact with the French agent REX.

The Polish codebreakers simply didn't have the resources to continue their assault on Enigma, so they invited cryptanalysts from Britain and France to visit their operation. The visitors thought Enigma was unbreakable and were astonished when Rejewski revealed that Polish intelligence had been breaking the code for years. He offered them replica Enigma machines and blueprints for making the *bomba*. These reached London just two weeks before the outbreak of war.

over. Further analysis would reveal the other letter pairs that had been swapped. Now Rejewski had the plugboard setting and the rotor settings – in other words, the complete day key. As the message key was enciphered by the day key at the beginning of each message, he could decrypt all the traffic that day. With the information received from France, it was now possible to work out the wiring of the rotors.

The *bomba*

Changes made by the Germans soon rendered Rejewski's catalogue of chain lengths useless. Rather than start another one, he devised a mechanical method of checking all possible rotor settings. It was essentially six Enigma machines – one with each of six arrangements of the rotors – working in parallel. The unit was a metre high and known as a *bomba*.

In December 1938, the Germans issued two more rotors, increasing the

Zygalski sheets

Rejewski spotted that sometimes there would be a repeated letter in the first and fourth, second and fifth, or third and sixth positions. These repeats were known as 'females'. It meant that a repeated letter in the plaintext message code had been transposed into the same letter in the ciphertext though the rotors were three steps ahead. This could only happen with certain initial settings of the rotors. The Polish team began cataloguing them.

Henryk Zygalski worked out a simple way to exploit this. He made up six sets of 26 sheets, one set for each possible order of the three rotors. Each sheet corresponded to one position of the left rotor. The alphabet along the top indicated the position of the middle rotor and the alphabet running down the side indicated the position of the right rotor. A hole was cut at the intersections where the rotor configuration would produce a female.

Rejewski explained: 'When the sheets were superposed and moved in the proper sequence and the proper manner with respect to each other, in accordance with a strictly defined programme, the number of visible apertures gradually decreased. And, if a sufficient quantity of data was available, there finally remained a single aperture, probably corresponding to the right case, that is, to the solution. From the position of the aperture one could calculate the order of the rotors, the setting of their rings, and, by comparing the letters of the cipher keys with the letters in the machine, likewise permutation S; in other words, the entire cipher key.'

The message code was preceded by an unenciphered three-letter indicator called the *Grundstellung*. The first letter indicated the position of the first rotor, so the cryptanalyst picked out the sheets with that letter for each of the messages found containing females in the message code. The horizontal and vertical offsets were given by the second and third letters of the indicator. Then the sheets were placed on the light table with the appropriate offsets.

The array of bombes would try all possible message codes until one rendered some legible plaintext in German.

Perforated Sheet
(figure 9)

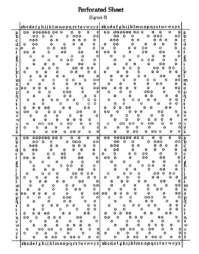

A Zygalski sheet was used to crack the early Enigma, but advances meant machines had to be used instead.

Where the holes fell on top of one another and the light could shine through, the analyst could read off the ring setting of the daily key. To make this work, each sheet had to have the alphabet written twice over along the top, sides and bottom, repeating the squares four times.

With just 12 females in a day's traffic, it was possible to narrow down the initial rotor settings to one or two. If there were two, it was possible to find out which was correct by deciphering the message through an Enigma machine. The false setting would yield gibberish, the right setting would give the plaintext.

On 15 December 1938, the Germans issued two more rotors for the Enigma machines. This meant Zygalski would need 60 sets of sheets rather than just six. At the meeting in July 1939, the Poles informed the British of the perforated sheet method of cracking Enigma. Sets were made up at Bletchley Park and sent to the Poles in France, where they were used to solve daily Enigma keys.

In 2011, a memorial to the Polish codebreakers was unveiled at Bletchley Park.

CHAPTER 9

BLETCHLEY PARK

'In the spring of 1941, Britain was losing the war. The German Wolf Packs were sinking the ships bringing in food and raw materials to Britain left, right and centre – and of course we didn't know where they were out there, waiting, lurking... Once naval Enigma was broken, the sinkings dropped by 75 per cent.'

Jerry Roberts
cryptographer, Bletchley Park

The Government Code and Cypher School was moved out of London to Bletchley Park in rural Buckinghamshire in 1938 to be safe from bombing. A top-secret establishment, known officially as Station X, it recruited an eccentric bunch of mathematicians, linguists, chess masters and crossword puzzlers, whose expertise in codebreaking helped win the war.

Bletchley Park, headquarters of Station X, the most secret site in Britain during World War II.

Cipher school

Britain's Government Code and Cypher School was formed in November 1919, initially under the auspices of the Admiralty and then the Foreign Office. Sir Hugh 'Quex' Sinclair, 'C' at the Secret Intelligence Service from 1923 to 1939, took charge and moved the school from its former home behind London's Charing Cross railway station, via distant Kensington, to its new headquarters at 54 Broadway, off Victoria Street, closer to both the Foreign Office and the Admiralty.

In 1924 a dedicated navy section was formed, while the rest of the school concentrated on diplomatic codes. An army section was formed in 1930 and an air force section in 1936. Until the eve of World War II, around 90 people worked there, some 30 of them cryptologists, while personnel from the armed services handled the intercepts.

First brush with Enigma

Alfred Dillwyn Knox (see box), an expert on the Greek poet Herodas who had helped break the Zimmermann telegram, concentrated on breaking the US codes, moving on to those used by Hungary. A former cryptanalyst for the Tsar broke the Soviet codes, while others read enciphered messages sent by the French, Italians, Spanish, Japanese and others. Since the introduction of the Enigma machine, they could not read German communications. It hardly mattered at first, as the size of the German armed forces had been limited by the Versailles Treaty and there was little message traffic.

Italy was perceived as a far greater danger. Dictator Benito Mussolini began

ALFRED DILLWYN KNOX (1884–1943)

A classicist who had once been tutor to future prime minister Harold Macmillan, Alfred Dillwyn 'Dilly' Knox became familiar with some of the techniques of cryptanalysis when piecing together the 'mimes' of Herodas from fragments of a papyrus lodged in the British Museum. The papyrus was a copy and the copyist was unfamiliar with the form of the letters he was copying. He made frequent mistakes and Knox was determined to reconstruct the original meanings.

Early in 1915, Knox was recruited to Room 40; his own office, Room 53, contained a huge table and a bathtub where he did much of his thinking. In 1920, he married Olive Rodham, who also worked at Room 40. After the war, Knox wanted to return to academic work, but Olive persuaded him to stay on with

GC&CS, where his work was of national importance.

In July 1939, Knox was one of the British delegation that flew to Poland to see, to their amazement, Rejewski's methods of breaking the Enigma code. The British 'were specialists of a different kind – of a different class,' said Rejewski. He also cleared up a matter which had been puzzling Knox for some time. With the commercial Enigma machine, the QWERTZUIO keyboard was wired, in order, to the 26 contacts on the entry ring – Q to the first contact, W to the second, E to the third, and so on. But from his analysis of intercepts from the military Enigma machine, Knox could see that the wiring had been changed and there were 26! (26x25x24... 3x2x1) or some 400 million million million million ways they could have done that. Rejewski told him that the Germans had simply rewired the connections in alphabetical order – A to the first contact, B to the second, C to the third . . . Knox was not so much shocked as disappointed.

When Knox returned to Britain, he wrote to Rejewski in Polish, enclosing a set of the batons or rods he had developed to break the commercial Enigma code.

'I don't know how Knox's method was supposed to work,' said Rejewski. 'Most likely he had hoped to vanquish Enigma with the batons. Unfortunately, we beat him to it.'

While Alan Turing (see page 119) was developing Rejewski's *bomba*, Knox continued to deploy his rodding method to break the ciphers used by the Italian Navy, leading to their defeat at the Battle of Cape Matapan in March 1941. Knox also cracked codes of the *Abwehr*, German military intelligence, who used a four-rotor Enigma machine with no plugboard. These decrypts provided information vital for the success of the Double Cross System of counter-intelligence (which captured or turned every German spy), and Operation Fortitude (which spread disinformation to deceive the Germans in the run-up to the D-Day landings).

calling the Mediterranean *mare nostrum* – 'our sea' – while for Britain it was the vital route to India. In 1935, Italy invaded Abyssinia, threatening British control of Egypt. The British soon realized that the Italian Navy was deciphering its messages using a commercial Enigma machine. Dilly Knox had bought one in Vienna in 1925, so the rotor wiring was known to GC&CS. The commercial machine had no plugboard, so Knox had to recover the daily code – the order in which the rotors

'If you get a message saying "today minus three", then you know that something pretty big is afoot. . . . It was eleven o'clock at night, and it was pouring with rain when I rushed, ran, absolutely tore down to take it to Intelligence, to get it across to Admiral Cunningham.'

Mavis Batey, cryptographer, on cracking a message to an Italian naval commander, Bletchley Park, 1941

were arranged – and the daily key, giving their starting positions.

It was possible to draw up a table for the three wheels, showing the possible transpositions for each position. The rows of letters in these tables (originally written along a strip of cardboard) were known as 'rods'. Certain transformations were impossible: a letter could not be transformed into itself; and two different letters could not be transformed into the same letter.

The Enigma machine both enciphered and deciphered, so if A enciphered as D, then D must encipher as A. Working with these exclusions, the cryptanalyst could narrow down the possibilities to what were known as 'rod couplings'.

It was then necessary to match a crib to pieces of ciphertext. To simplify matters, Knox realized that until the turning of the right-hand or 'fast' wheel tripped the middle ring, moving it on a space, they were dealing with a simple two-stage transposition cipher. The letters on the keyboard of the commercial Enigma connected to the entry ring that made contact with the first rotor. The wiring of the rotor then changed one letter into another. As the other rotors and the reflector remained static, they acted as a virtual reflector, making one further substitution.

Using his rodding method, Knox began to break the codes used by the forces of General Franco and the German personnel sent to Spain. Then the German Navy joined the fray and

Benito Mussolini, Fascist dictator of Italy.

THE BLETCHLEY GIRLS

A large number of young women, often debutantes, were recruited to Bletchley Park. They were officially Wrens – members of the Women's Royal Naval Service. However, among them were a number of top-flight mathematicians. Joan Clarke worked closely with Alan Turing and went on to become deputy head of Hut 8. After the war, she remained with GCHQ until she retired in 1977. Assistant to Dilly Knox, Mavis Batey helped break the Italian Navy code before the Battle of Matapan. She also broke a message between Belgrade and Berlin, enabling Knox's team to work out the wiring of the Abwehr Enigma.

Margaret Rock also worked on breaking the Abwehr Enigma, which played a vital role in the success of the D-Day landings. She remained with GCHQ until she retired in 1963. Jane Hughes was head of team of the women in Hut 6 who decoded a message giving the position of the German battleship *Bismarck*, which was sunk by the Royal Navy two days later.

---

they were using military Enigma machines with plugboards and he was stymied.

Breaking the Italian Navy code

Rodding could still be used to break the Italian Navy code. Knox employed a group of young women to do the donkey work and suggested they look for messages beginning with 'FOR' ('PER' in Italian) followed by a space marked with an X.

Mavis Batey, an 18-year-old German student at London University said: 'This went on tediously and unsuccessfully for months until finally when S, rejecting X, appeared of its own accord from the first coupling. I did not disregard the position but decided PERSONALE might pay off as a guess. It did.'

There was enough ciphertext left before the turning of the first rotor moved the next one on and Mavis discovered that the message began: PERSONALEXPERXSIGNORX followed by a name. This was enough to identify the day's rotor order and the message setting for the signal she had been rodding. Once some of the Italian Navy Enigma messages could be read, they provided useful cribs which could be used to break the cipher on subsequent days. For the time being, the Italian Navy Enigma had been broken.

The move to Bletchley

As war approached and GC&CS expanded, Sinclair realized that his codebreakers would need both quiet and secrecy. The British government bought a Victorian manor house at Bletchley Park, some 80km (50 miles) northwest of London. With easy access by train from London, Oxford and Cambridge, it was ideally situated and surrounded by acres of rolling countryside, ensuring adequate security.

The house itself was not large enough to accommodate the personnel required, so wooden huts were built in the grounds. Knox moved into a small cottage that had formerly been the servants' quarters and went to work on Enigma with the machines the Polish cryptographers had provided.

Hut 6 at Bletchley Park, where the German Army and Air Force Enigma was broken.

Soon after the codebreakers moved to Bletchley, the German battleship SMS *Schleswig-Holstein* sailed into the harbour at Danzig, ostensibly to mark the 25th anniversary of the sinking of the *Magdeburg*, whose dead had been buried there. Instead, at 4.48 a.m. on the morning of 1 September 1939, she turned her main battery on a Polish military depot, firing the first shots of World War II.

Rejewski, Rózycki and Zygalski fled to France where, in short order, they broke the Germany army key for 28 October 1939, then the air force codes for 6 January 1940.

More mathematicians

The head of GC&CS, Alastair Denniston, had already taken a leaf out of the Poles' book. Instead of hiring more classicists such as Knox, he realized that codebreaking in the modern, mechanized era required mathematicians.

One of the first to be employed was 27-year-old prodigy Alan Turing (see box). After a course in cryptology at GC&CS's headquarters at Broadway Buildings, he joined Knox to work on Enigma along with other recruits, including Oxford mathematician Peter Twinn.

Turing was largely concerned with mathematical theory. He had built an electric multiplying machine while a PhD student at Princeton University in the USA, so took an immediate interest in the Polish *bomba*. He recognized immediately that, like Knox's rods, rejecting all possible inconsistencies drastically narrowed down the possibilities that had to be tested.

Turing thought the Germans would soon spot the weakness of enciphering the message key twice at the beginning, but reasoned that other cribs could be used. These would have to be tested against the entire message, so the machinery checking for inconsistencies would need to run a lot faster than the *bomba*. Turing came up with his own design for a new, more complex version, known as a bombe, and employed the British Tabulating Machine Company to make it.

ALAN TURING (1912–54)

Winston Churchill credited Alan Turing with making the single biggest contribution to the Allied victory over Nazi Germany in World War II. Turing was an unworldly Cambridge mathematician, careless about his appearance and diffident in his manner, but no one could doubt his genius. He became a fellow of King's College at the age of just 22. Two years later, he had laid the intellectual foundation of modern computing, outlining what became known as the Universal Turing Machine in 1936. During a sojourn at Princeton, he began to make components.

In 1938, he returned to Britain and, the following year, joined the wartime headquarters of the Government Code and Cypher School at Bletchley Park in Buckinghamshire. His task there was to break the German Enigma code.

When the Polish cryptanalysts demonstrated their *bomba* at a conference near Warsaw in July 1939, Turing was particularly impressed. However, in May 1940 a change in German procedures rendered the *bomba* virtually useless.

This was when the genius of Turing came into play. He developed the *bomba* further, calling his British version a 'bombe'. He then took what he called a crib – a phrase that was likely to appear in an intercepted radio message – and ran it using all possible rotor settings until the intercepted ciphertext appeared. This gave the codebreakers that day's key and allowed them to read all of the messages transmitted that day.

Cribs would come from captured documents, messages sent in plaintext, the interrogations of prisoners, and guesses based on recent events. It was surprising how often messages signed off with the words 'Heil Hitler', or bored radio operators posted: 'Nothing special to report.' The first British bombe was installed at Bletchley Park on 18 March 1940.

continued on next page

continued from previous page

During the ensuing Battle of Britain, Bletchley Park concentrated on breaking the German air force codes. This was relatively easy as *Luftwaffe* signalmen were not properly trained and often used their girlfriends' names for a key setting. Messages from *Luftwaffe* liaison officers provided valuable information about army operations.

However, the German Navy employed a different system. It used a book of random keys that were themselves encrypted. It was vital to get hold of one of those books. This was done with a series of 'pinches' where the Royal Navy managed to board a German vessel and seize the codes before they could be destroyed.

These codebooks allowed Turing's team to decipher within a few hours of interception the messages sent by the 'wolf packs' of U-boats which were harassing Allied shipping. Consequently the Allied convoys were able to avoid concentrations of enemy submarines at the very moment at which war planners predicted Britain was to face starvation.

Along with the codebooks, Bletchley Park had accumulated a large cache of cribs from German naval terminology, orders and reports. The number of bombes grew until the codebreakers could decipher over 80,000 messages a month. Turing's bombes continued to yield vital intelligence for the rest of the war. He went on to design the electronic computer at the National Physical Laboratory, then moved to the Computing Machine Laboratory at the University of Manchester, home of the world's first electronic stored-program digital computer. There he worked on artificial intelligence and developed the 'Turing test', the criterion for whether a computer can think.

In March 1952, Turing was prosecuted for homosexuality, then against the law, and sentenced to 12 months of hormone therapy – known colloquially as 'chemical castration'. In June 1954, he was found dead from cyanide poisoning. He had been using cyanide for silver-plating teaspoons. The coroner's verdict was suicide, though no motive was ever discovered.

Victory

On 10 March 1940, just before the German Army moved westwards into the Low Countries, they stopped using the double message key and their communications were, again, unreadable. A week later, Turning's first bombe, named Victory, arrived at Bletchley Park

It was 2m (6½ ft) tall, 2.2m (7ft) long and 0.6m (2ft) wide, and weighed over a ton. Inside were thirty-six 'scramblers', each emulating an Enigma machine, and 108 drums selecting the possible key settings. Like the Polish model, it narrowed the possibilities for chains. The drums span round until a circuit was made. At that point, the machine shuddered to a halt and the settings were read off. These were then used to set up a replica Enigma machine to see if plaintext in German came out. If it did not, the machine was restarted. Unless the crib was long – over 150 letters – there were a large number of false stops. To run a single crib in all wheel orders took a week.

A recreation of the World War II Operations Room at Bletchley Park.

Diagonal board

The Cambridge mathematician Gordon Welchman (see box on page 124) devised a modification which speeded things up. This was the 'diagonal board'. Enigma substitutions were reciprocal. If plaintext 'p' was enciphered as B, then 'b' would be enciphered as P on the same settings. Welchman produced a board with 676 contacts lettered A–Z across the top and A–Z down the side. He then connected row B, column E to row E, column B, making all possible reciprocal connections. When 'r' in the crib was tested against D in the ciphertext, plaintext 'd' was automatically tested against ciphertext R. This cut down the number of erroneous stops. Turing realized that it allowed them to do simultaneous scanning of all possible plugboard settings.

The second bombe, known as 'Agnus Dei' or 'Lamb of God' or, colloquially, 'Aggie', arrived in August 1940 with Welchman's diagonal board fitted, as did all subsequent models. Turing then discovered that the finding of rotor and plug settings could be further speeded up. Sometimes, during the encryption of one message, the rotors would be in the same position as the starting position of another message. To find these matches, the intercepts were transferred to large index cards with the alphabet printed in columns. The letters of the message were then punched out, column by column. When one card was moved over another on a lightbox it was possible to spot these repeats. As the cards were printed in Banbury, Oxfordshire, this method was known as 'Banburismus'.

Throughout the Battle of Britain, July–September 1940, the team at Bletchley Park was breaking German air force codes and relaying the intelligence to RAF fighter pilots. But slower progress was being made with German Navy codes, and U-boat attacks on Allied shipping threated to starve Britain of food and munitions.

Navy codes

The German Navy supplied three more rotors – VI, VII and VIII. Using a different three each time increased the possible order from 60 to 336. This gave a staggering 6,0 17,675,512,800,000,000,000,000 possible settings. Worse still, the messages were then super-enciphered. The output of the Enigma machine was encoded a second time, this time by hand using 'bigram tables', which Turing set about reconstructing.

The German operator would pick three letters at random as the starting positions for the rotors – ASC, say. These would be enciphered twice using the daily settings, so ASCASC would become, perhaps, LQRCPY. To disguise them further, the operator would write them in this pattern:

L Q R
  C P Y

Two letters would be chosen at random to complete the rectangle, giving:

L Q R T
O C P Y

The operator would encrypt the vertical digraphs LO, QC, RP and TY using the bigram tables. There were ten of these in use for up to a year. The one to be used was given in the daily settings. LO might become TU, QC might become AH, RP might become LS and TY might become IU. The rectangle would be:

T A L I
U H S U

By the time the Battle of Britain had started the codebreakers at Bletchley Park were reading Luftwaffe Enigma messages, so they knew when an attack was coming.

GORDON WELCHMAN (1906–85)

After gaining a first in mathematics at Trinity College, Cambridge, Gordon Welchman became a fellow of Sidney Sussex College in 1929. Invited to Bletchley Park by Knox, and armed with a handful of Enigma intercepts that had already been solved, he was assigned to low-level work on call signs, address indicators and frequencies used. Welchman quickly realized he was dealing with an entire communication system that would serve the needs of the German ground and air forces, and he developed the vital intelligence tool of traffic analysis.

After independently devising a system of decryption using perforated sheets, Welchman devised the diagonal board which, added to Turing's bombes, speeded up finding the keys. When the war ended, he became director of research at the John Lewis Partnership before moving to the United States where he taught the first computer course at MIT. He went on to join the federally funded Mitre Corporation and worked on secure communications for the US military, becoming a US citizen in 1962. The authorities tried to stop him publishing his wartime memoirs, *The Hut Six Story*, in 1982 and his accreditation to the Mitre Corporation was withdrawn.

The operator would transmit TALI UHSU and the German recipient would then reverse the procedure. The bigram tables were reciprocal, so if LO becomes TU, then TU becomes LO. After eliminating the two added letters, it was easy to check there was no mistake. Once deciphered, the first three letters were repeated. They would then be used by both sender and receiver to set the rotors. This added a whole new level of difficulty for the codebreakers.

Undaunted, Alan Turing and Hut 8 set to work on the Navy Enigma. His deputy, Hugh Alexander, said: 'In the early days, he was the only cryptographer who thought the problem worth tackling and not only was he primarily responsible for the main theoretical work within the Hut (particularly the development of a satisfactory scoring technique for dealing with Banburismus) but he also shared with Welchman and Keen the chief credit for the invention of the bombe... the pioneer work always tends to be forgotten when experience and routine later make everything seem easy and many of us in Hut 8 felt that the magnitude of Turing's contribution was never fully realized by the outside world.'

German U-boats were doing so much damage to the Atlantic convoys that Britain faced starvation, until Turing and Hut 8 broke the naval Enigma.

Pinches

Many of the advances were made with 'pinches', where happenstance brought German machines and codebooks into Allied hands. One such incident occurred on the morning of 26 April 1940, when HMS *Griffin* intercepted a fishing boat named *Polares* sailing under a Dutch flag south of Trondheim and discovered it was carrying munitions. In fact, it was the disguised German trawler, *Schiff 26*. One of the boarding party noticed a canvas bag in the water and jumped in to retrieve it, almost drowning in the process. In it were found the operator's log book containing messages in plaintext – perfect cribs – and the plugboard settings and starting positions for 23–24 April. Using these, Turing's team in Hut 8 managed to crack six days' traffic.

OPERATION RUTHLESS

In September 1940, an audacious plan to get hold of the German naval codes was put forward by a Royal Navy Intelligence officer named Lieutenant Commander Ian Fleming, later the creator of James Bond. It was called 'Operation Ruthless'. His idea was to crash a captured German bomber into the Channel. When a German ship came to the rescue, the British crew would seize it, kill its crew and take the vessel along with its codebooks and Enigma machine back to an English port. The plan was cancelled when reconnaissance planes could find no suitable German shipping in the Channel.

Then, on the morning of 4 March 1941, HMS *Somali* found itself in a gun battle off Norway's Lofoten Islands with an armed German trawler named *Krebs*. The trawler was quickly disabled. On board were found boxes containing two rotors, along with a document giving the plugboard and rotor settings for February. Even though they were out-of-date, they were useful for Turing's reconstruction of the bigram tables.

As the Bletchley team slowly deciphered old messages, 22-year-old Harry Hinsley noted that German trawlers were being sent to a position north of Iceland to send back weather reports. It dawned on him that these unprotected weatherships must be carrying Enigma machines and codebooks. On 7 May, HMS *Somali* and HMS *Edinburgh* intercepted the *München*. The crew threw the Enigma machine and codebooks overboard before she was boarded, but the British did manage to capture the settings for June.

On 9 May, the day before the documents from the *München* reached Bletchley Park, the German U-boat *U-110* attacked a British convoy. Depth charges forced her to the surface. When she was boarded by the British, they found an Enigma machine set up for use together with codebooks. The captured documents included the bigram tables that Turing had been reconstructing. They confirmed his work.

Ultra

By June, Bletchley Park were able to decode all the German naval traffic almost as fast as the Germans themselves. The details were passed to the government as 'Ultra'. Breaking the Navy Enigma proved decisive. Downing Street war planners had predicted that German U-boat packs would have torpedoed Britain into starvation by June 1941. Surrender would have been inevitable and the war lost. 'The only thing that ever really frightened me during the war was the U-boat peril,' Churchill said later.

With information supplied by Ultra, the supply convoys plying the Atlantic could be steered away from the wolf packs. Losses fell dramatically and, for 23 days straight, the U-boats never even sighted a convoy.

There was always a danger that the Germans would realize their code had been broken and their messages read, so disinformation was spread that the British had developed a new long-range radar which could detect submarines even when they were underwater.

In 1942, when five Italian ships carrying supplies to Axis forces in North Africa were sunk as the result of information from Ultra, Churchill sent a telegram to Naples congratulating a fictitious spy there. This proved to be unnecessary, as the paranoid Nazi regime had already assumed some spy was passing details of U-boat movements to the British.

Besides, in the summer of 1941, U-boats deployed in the Atlantic had been shifted to the Mediterranean. Those remaining had orders not to sink American shipping. As Hitler began his invasion of the Soviet Union, he did not want to risk provoking the USA into declaring war as well. But Churchill knew the difference the codebreakers had made: 'It was thanks to Ultra,' he told King George VI later, 'that we won the war.'

Action this day

On 6 September, Churchill visited Bletchley Park to thank the codebreakers himself and was introduced to Turing, Welchman and Alexander. He was shocked at the dishevelled state of his top cryptanalysts, saying to Sir Stewart Menzies, then head of SIS: 'I know I told you to leave no stone unturned to find the necessary staff, but I didn't mean you to take me so literally.'

The complex naval Enigma had been broken, but the cryptological war was far from over. On 21 October, the anniversary of the Battle of Trafalgar, Turing, Welchman, Alexander and Welchman's deputy, Stuart Milner-Barry (see box on page 129), wrote to Churchill, saying:

'Dear Prime Minister,

'Some weeks ago you paid us the honour of a visit, and we believe that you regard our work as important. You will have seen that... we have been well supplied with the "bombes" for the breaking of the German Enigma codes. We think, however, that you ought to know that this work is being held up, and in some cases is not being done at all, principally because we cannot get sufficient staff to deal with it. Our reason for writing to you direct is that for months we have done everything that we possibly can through the normal channels, and we despair of any early improvement without your intervention.'

Churchill's immediate response was a memo that read:

'Action this Day

'Make sure they have all they want on extreme priority and report to me that this has been done.'

Bletchley Park was going to need all the help it could get. In February, the German Navy introduced a new, modified Enigma machine. Their cryptography department had slimmed down the reflector, making room for a fourth rotor inside the machine. There were two versions, named beta and gamma, as they were not interchangeable with the other broader rotors. What was needed was another pinch.

On 30 October 1942, U-559 was sighted in the eastern Mediterranean.

HMS *Petard* was one of five destroyers to give chase. Depth charges forced the submarine to the surface. Two of the boarding party drowned when the disabled U-boat suddenly sank, but they had already recovered a new version of the weather-report book that provided important new cribs. Hut 8 didn't break the new four-rotor Enigma until 2 December 1942, when it was discovered that, for short messages, the fourth wheel had been set to A with its ring setting at Z. This meant that the existing three-rotor bombes could break the short intercepts. From there, it was relatively simple to work out the fourth rotor settings for longer messages.

Meanwhile, Hut 6 had been busy deciphering traffic intercepted in North Africa. Their findings gave Britain its first victory in World War II at El-Alamein in Egypt, in a battle that raged from 23 October to 4 November 1942.

After Japan's attack on Pearl Harbor on 7 December 1941, Hitler declared war on the USA. Britain and the United States were now allies and American cryptanalysts visited Bletchley Park, bringing with them a 'Purple' machine which they had used to crack the Japanese codes (see page 136).

Turing was sent to America where he went to work in Bell Labs in Manhattan after having been given security clearance from the White House. He also visited the US Navy codebreaking unit in Washington, D.C. and the National Cash Register Corporation in Dayton, Ohio, which was making bombes for the Americans. By the end of 1943, the codebreaking of Mediterranean intercepts was handed over to Washington. Even so, the increased communications traffic meant that Bletchley Park had to accommodate its growing numbers of bombes in outstations up to 30 miles away.

HMS Petard *had the distinction of sinking a submarine from each of the three Axis navies: Germany's U-559; Italy's Uarsciek; and Japan's I-27.*

HUGH ALEXANDER (1909–74)

After gaining a first in mathematics at Cambridge University, Hugh Alexander became director of research at the John Lewis Partnership. He was in Buenos Aires with the British chess team when war broke out. Early in 1940, he joined Turing in Hut 8. One of his colleagues there said: 'Alexander is one of the most intelligent people I've known, and I've known a lot of intelligent people.'

When Turing left Bletchley Park to liaise with cryptanalysts in the US, Alexander took over as head of Hut 8. Then, in December 1944, he moved on to cracking the Japanese naval codes and was posted to HMS *Anderson*, the Signals Intelligence station in Ceylon (Sri Lanka), in the summer of 1945.

After the war he returned, briefly, to the John Lewis Partnership, before rejoining the GC&CS, then reformed as the Government Communications Headquarters (GCHQ). He also became the chess correspondent of the *Sunday Times*, the *Financial Times*, the *Evening News* and *The Spectator*.

The British chess team at the Buenos Aires Olympiad 1939 (from left to right): B.H. Wood, Sir Stuart Milner-Barry, Vera Menchik, Sir George Thomas, Hugh Alexander and Harry Golombek.

STUART MILNER-BARRY (1906–95)

A classics student at Cambridge, Stuart Milner-Barry became a stockbroker in the City of London, composing chess puzzles in his spare time. In 1938, he became the chess correspondent of *The Times*. He was in Buenos Aires with Hugh Alexander and the British chess team when war broke out in 1939. When the two men joined GC&CS at Bletchley Park, they were billeted together at the Shoulder of Mutton pub.

Milner-Barry was Gordon Welchman's deputy at Hut 6 and took over as head in 1943, maintaining its ability to decipher German traffic despite fresh modifications of the Enigma machine. After the war, he joined the Treasury, later administering the honours system. He continued playing championship chess and was president of the British Chess Federation from 1970 to 1973.

CHAPTER 10

RED AND PURPLE

'I'd never seen Americans before, except in the films. I just plied them with sherry. I hadn't the faintest idea what they were doing there; I wasn't told.'

Barbara Abernethy,
personal assistant to Alistair Denniston,
Bletchley Park

The Japanese realized that the United States had broken their codes, so began electro-mechanical cryptology along the lines of Germany's Enigma. As war in the Pacific loomed, US codebreakers strived to keep pace. Despite the isolationists, the United States sought renewed cooperation with British codebreakers as President Roosevelt feared that being dragged into a war with Germany was inevitable.

The Pentagon building, headquarters of the United States Department of Defense.

US intelligence and Japanese codes

With the closing of the Black Chamber, the United States War Department was left with just one cryptanalyst, William F. Friedman. The following year, he was allowed to hire three junior cryptanalysts at $2,000. They were schoolmasters who taught mathematics and knew nothing about codebreaking. In 1938, he was permitted to hire another three 'cryptographic clerks' with a salary of $1,440. One of them, John B. Hurt, had taught himself Japanese without ever setting foot in Japan. Once, when hit by a taxi, the driver stopped to ask him: 'Are you hurt?' 'Yes,' he replied. 'John B.'

With a slowly expanding budget, Friedman hired four civil servants from other agencies, two men and two women. One of them, Frank Lewis, was chosen on the basis that he played bridge and chess, and wrote cryptic crossword puzzles.

The Japanese Red and two-part enciphered Blue codes – so called because of the colours of the binders that recovered code groups were stored in – had long since been broken, largely through 'black-bag' operations where agents break into security buildings to steal or photograph codebooks and other material. But there would soon be plenty for the staff of the Signal Intelligence Service (SIS) to do.

The Signal Intelligence Service (SIS) was established in 1929 to control all army cryptologic activity. In this photo are Friedman (centre, standing) and the SIS staff in 1935. This small but talented group ultimately broke the Japanese diplomatic machine.

WILLIAM F. FRIEDMAN (1891–1969)

William F. Friedman born in Russia of Jewish parents and arrived in the USA at the age of one. After studying at Michigan Agricultural College and Cornell, he was hired by George Fabyan to head the Department of Genetics at his Riverbank Laboratories in 1915. Another of Fabyan's pet projects was to prove that Francis Bacon had written the works of William Shakespeare, and Friedman helped search the text of the plays for hidden ciphers. He married another cryptographer on the project, Elizabeth Smith, who went on to become senior cryptanalyst at the US Treasury, breaking the codes used by bootleggers and drug smugglers.

With the outbreak of World War I, US Army officers were sent to Riverbank to be taught cryptology by Friedman who, by then, had produced a number of monographs on the subject. Enlisting in the army, he went to France as General Pershing's personal cryptographer. In 1921, he became the chief cryptographer at the War Department, later heading the Signal Intelligence Service during World War II.

After the war, he became head of the cryptographic division of the newly formed Armed Forces Security Agency. In 1952, he became chief cryptologist at the National Security Agency (NSA) where he made a secret agreement with Crypto AG, the Swiss manufacturer of cipher machines, so that the NSA could read their output.

In his spare time Friedman tried to decipher the Voynich manuscript (see page 52). After his retirement in 1956, he returned to searching for ciphers in Shakespeare.

The cipher machines

Following revelations about the NSA published in Herbert Yardley's *The American Black Chamber* in 1931, the Japanese realized their codes were vulnerable. They introduced a cipher machine, known in the West as 'Red'. Much simpler than the Enigma machine, it was broken independently by the British and the Americans. The task had been made easy for them, as Red machines used the Roman alphabet with Japanese transliterated into what was called *romaji*. This was broken into 'sixes and twenties' – vowels were enciphered as vowels and consonants as consonants, with Y counting as a vowel. The vowels occurred frequently in *romaji* and basically formed a six-by-six Vigenère table; the consonants formed a 20-by-20 table. Both shifted down one key position as each letter was typed in. The options for setting up the machine were limited and SIS discovered that the pattern of stepping through the Vignenère table always followed a cycle of 41, 42, or 43.

On 20 February 1939, a new machine which SIS would dub 'Purple' appeared. It was much more complicated, being enciphered on a device adapted from an Enigma machine lent by the Germans. Then, on 1 June, new codebooks were issued. The codebreakers called the new code 'JN-25', as it was the twenty-fifth Japanese Navy system identified.

For some time, Japanese diplomats continued using Red machines, providing valuable cribs. The Japanese tended to spell out the message number at the beginning of every despatch. Detailed logs of the traffic from each station gave the first few words of the message.

A team working under Frank Rowlett at the SIS quickly discovered that Purple still separated the alphabet into sixes and twenties, but vowels were no longer enciphered as vowels, and consonants as consonants. The six were selected by a plugboard, connecting them to one scrambler. The other 20 letters were connected to another plugboard.

The connections were changed daily, but could easily be determined, as with Red, by

The Purple machine, based on the German Enigma.

designed for automatic telephone exchanges would do the job. This had six switches ganged together which swept around 25 contacts. It was not until the war was over that the Americans discovered the Purple machine used a similar bank of stepping switches.

While the sixes were soon cracked, it was not until a year later that Genevieve Grotjan, one of the civil servants Friedman had hired, spotted that cyclical patterns were generated that were 25 key positions long. They were generated by three banks of four uniselectors each. These three banks could be set to fast, medium or slow, just like the three rotors in the Enigma machine – and so were vulnerable to the same cryptanalysis. It was necessary to work out the substitution tables for the three scramblers.

frequency analysis. The six letters selected were scrambled among themselves, but still their frequency would be the same as the plaintext. That worked for the twenties too.

The sixes could be worked out in a 6-by-25 table, using paper and pencil. This was a slow, clumsy business and Rowlett realized there had to be a better way to do it using IBM tabulating machines and punch cards.

Ganged switches

What was needed was a device that connected the six input letters to the six output letters in the 25 different ways required. Leo Rosen, an electrical engineer from MIT and newly recruited to SIS, thought a 'uniselector'

SIS was based in the Munitions Building in Washington, DC. In late summer, it was hot and humid and there was no air-conditioning. As the US prepared for war, the building was being expanded, with the addition of an extra floor. The cryptanalyst could either swelter in the heat with the windows closed, or suffer the noise of the building work with the windows open. Nevertheless, in three weeks the job was done.

Again, it was Rosen's job to find a mechanical way of handling the decryption. He began the task of wiring up banks of

> 'As there was not much traffic, the [first intercepted Red] messages were put into one of those "to be looked at when there is nothing else to do" bins.'
>
> Cryptologic Quarterly, 1984

THE PURPLE MACHINE

The *97-shiki O-bun In-ji-ki*, or Alphabetical Typewriter '97', was codenamed 'Purple' by the US military. It was usually referred to by the Japanese as 'the machine', though the Imperial Japanese Navy called it 'J'. They had adapted it from a German Enigma machine. It was called 'alphabetical' because it used *romaji*, the transliteration of Japanese into the Roman alphabet. The '97' came from year 2597 of the Japanese calendar, which corresponds to 1937.

The device sat in a box between two Underwood electric typewriters, connected to them by 26 wires and a plugboard. To operate it, the cipher clerk would consult a book giving the daily keys, then set up the plugboard and turn the four discs in the scrambler to the given numbers. The message was then typed in and it printed out in cipher. The same process was used to decipher messages.

uniselectors to the keyboard from a prototype SIGABA machine. Thousands of connections had to be soldered. Men from the Signals Corps undertook this work in shifts.

Eventually, the task was complete. Rowlett then typed the ciphertext of a Purple intercept into the keyboard and out of the printer came plaintext in *romaji*.

The SIGABA machine.

THE SIGABA MACHINE

In 1921, American businessman Edward H. Hebern designed a rotor-based cipher machine which generated some interest from the US Navy. It went into production, but sales were slow and Hebern's company went bust; but the Navy took up his ideas and the first Electric Cipher Machine went into service in 1939. At the SIS, Friedman added a paper tape reader to randomize the movement of the rotors. He and Rowlett continued the machine's development until they had a device with five rotors taking their input from an electric typewriter. However, after this was introduced as the M-134-A, Friedman decided that the ECM was superior. After the Japanese air attack on Pearl Harbor, the US Navy adopted the ECM, while the army took the M-134-C, or SIGABA.

The daily task

There was still the daily task of finding the starting point of each of the four uniselectors. But of the 25^4 (or 390,625) possible positions, the Japanese utilized only 240. Using cribs from message numbers and punctuation at the beginning of the despatches, it was discovered that of the 26! (or 400,000,000,000,000) possible pluggings only around a thousand were ever used. Tables were drawn up.

The cryptanalysts had plenty of cribs to fall back on, especially when Purple was adopted by the Japanese Foreign Office. The diplomats tended to use standard phrases such as: 'I have the honour to inform Your Excellency. . .', and they liked to number paragraphs. Reading the Japanese newspapers also gave an idea of the subjects of the intercepts; the State Department often published the full text of diplomatic notes from the Japanese government which had been intercepted when sent, enciphered, to the Japanese Embassy in Washington, DC.

Magic

The cryptanalysts were in business and the Purple decrypts were circulated under the codename 'Magic'. Circulation was restricted to the President, the Secretaries of State, War and the Navy, the Chief of Staff, the Chief of Naval Operations, the heads of the army and navy war plans divisions and the heads of the army and navy intelligence divisions – a total of ten people initially. Others did get to see the intercepts, but field commanders were specifically excluded. However, information from intercepts was fed to them and attributed to a 'highly reliable source'.

There was then a turf war between the army and navy about who should deal with Purple intercepts of diplomatic traffic. It was eventually decided that the army's SIS should handle them on even-numbered days, while on odd-numbered days intercepts would be dealt with by OP-20-G – that is, the Office of Chief of Naval Operations (OPNAV), 20th Division of the Office of Naval Communications, G Section/Communications Security. In practice, though, the army and navy often cooperated.

Navy cryptanalyst Lieutenant Francis A. Raven spotted there was a relationship between the daily keys of each of the three ten-day sections of the month. It seemed that the cryptographer providing them had simply taken the first day's key and shuffled the order. So once the codebreakers had cracked the first day's key they had no problem reading the intercepts for the next nine days.

Vital military intelligence

The SIS grew worried when Henry Stimson was appointed Secretary of War and closed down the Black Chamber (see page 85). But he visited to see the Purple machine they had built and explained that the situation in 1940 was very different from the one they had faced in 1929. With the rest of the world already at war, military intelligence was vital.

Although the United States had yet to enter the war, a US mission under Brigadier General George V. Strong was sent to talk to the British. Strong proposed an exchange of information on cryptography.

The intelligence services on both sides were sceptical at first, especially as the Americans knew that the British had been trying to break their codes. Despite this, the SIS gave the British the solution to Purple.

On the British side, though, GC&CS head Alexander Denniston insisted on certain conditions. The chiefs of the various UK intelligence services agreed that, when American liaison officers arrived, they should be steered away from work on Enigma and be given only low-level material where their assistance could be valuable. After all, the USA was not at war and, remaining officially neutral, it still had diplomatic contact with the Axis powers.

Friedman was scheduled to be sent to the UK, but he suffered a nervous breakdown. Instead, the SIS sent Abe Sinkov, one of Friedman's original 1930s intake, and Leo Rosen, along with two lieutenants from the US Navy. Their mission was top secret, as American isolationists were fighting a last-ditch battle in the Senate over the Lend-Lease bill (a proposal to provide food and

munitions to the UK to aid the war effort), and aviator Charles Lindbergh was still advocating a neutrality pact with Germany.

The American codebreakers were to travel in plain clothes on board the British battleship *King George V*, which had just arrived at Annapolis carrying the new British ambassador, Lord Halifax. They brought with them a Purple machine, a Japanese typewriter and documents. Along the way, the crates carrying them were shot up by a German plane, but their precious cargo was undamaged.

At Bletchley Park, the Americans were passed off as a Canadian delegation. While they were there, Congress passed the Lend-Lease Act and Churchill agreed that Bletchley Park should let them into the secrets of solving Enigma, although they were not to be shown any of the actual decrypts. The Americans were required to sign secrecy agreements saying that they would only pass on what they had learned by word of mouth – and only to their immediate superiors. No written notes were to be taken. In exchange, the British handed over Purple intercepts from the Far East Bureau in Hong Kong and, later, Singapore.

Cooperation

In Hut 6, Lieutenant Colonel John Tiltman had cracked the Enigma code used by the German railways and learned

Charles A. Lindbergh, who made the first nonstop solo flight across the Atlantic, campaigned to keep America out of World War II.

of the preparations being made for the invasion of Greece and the Soviet Union. This was confirmed by a Purple decrypt of a message sent by General Oshima Hiroshi, the Japanese ambassador to Berlin, reporting that Hitler had told him that 'in all probability war with Russia cannot be avoided'. The US added its warnings to those sent to Stalin by Churchill. But Stalin refused to listen and was still sending raw material to Germany only hours before German soldiers began their invasion of the Soviet Union at 3 a.m. on 22 June 1941.

Churchill immediately began sending Ultra intelligence to Moscow. Denniston protested; given the insecurity of Soviet field ciphers, he said, 'it would only be a matter of days before the Germans would know of our success, and operations in the future would almost certainly be hidden

in an unbreakable way'. He insisted on personally approving every message sent to Moscow. Those he let through were attributed to a 'most reliable source'.

Through Enigma decrypts, the British began to learn of atrocities as the Germans pushed forwards into Soviet territory, particularly the rounding up and shooting of large numbers of commissars and Jews. Tiltman also broke the ciphers used by the German police. Through these, the British began to learn of the Holocaust, as Jews in Germany were rounded up and shipped to the death camps. Bletchley Park began a file for possible use in future war crimes trials, though captured documents and eyewitness statements were more than enough to convict Nazi war criminals at Nuremberg. Bletchley Park's file remained closed until 1996.

When Germany turned on the Soviet Union in 1941, Britain was unsure of how much Ultra information it could entrust to its new ally.

CHAPTER 11

THE JAPANESE NAVAL CODES

*'Roosevelt's personal bonhomie was based on
a shrewd appreciation that Britain must not
be allowed to lose the war. . . that she must be
humoured until the United States was strong
enough to take over the direction of the war and
wage it as she thought fit.'*

Michael Howard,
historian, *Times Literary Supplement,*
autumn 2009

**It became clear to US cryptologists and
the government officials who read their
decrypts that Japan intended to attack
the USA, but constant changes in the
Japanese naval codes made it impossible
to tell where the attack would come.**

*A view of smoke billowing from the aircraft carrier the USS
Wasp following hits from three torpedoes launched by the Japanese
submarine I-19, Pacific Ocean, 15 September 1942.*

JN-25

Although Purple had been broken, Japan's chief command and control communications JN-25 code had not. The SIS and OP-20-G attacked it with the IBM tabulators. Little progress was made until someone at OP-20-G remembered that the old Japanese 'S' code, which had been stolen some years earlier, assigned four-digit code groups to numbers. Zero was 0000, 1 was 0102, 2 was 0204, 3 was 0306, and so on. This was important, as messages often began with a reference to a previous message, giving its number.

Using a method of differences, cryptanalysts spotted that 00102, 00204, 00306 and 00408 kept coming up. After a year of trying, they had discovered the code groups for all the numbers from zero to 999. Another clue was that a safeguard had been written into the code to prevent it being garbled: the sum of the digits in each code group was divisible by three.

While at Bletchley Park, the American delegation discovered that the British were making progress on another part of JN-25 in the Far East. Immediately, results and liaison officers were exchanged between the Far East Bureau in Singapore and the US Navy's cryptanalytic unit at Cavite Naval Base in the Philippines. But just as progress was being made, the Japanese updated their codes yet again; preparations for their attack on Pearl Harbor were underway.

The Combat Intelligence Unit

In June 1941, Lieutenant Commander Joseph J. Rochefort was sent to take over the Radio Unit of the 14th Naval District

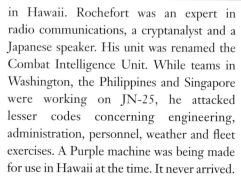

JOSEPH J. ROCHEFORT (1900–76)

Joseph Rochefort joined the US Navy from high school. Gifted at solving crossword puzzles and playing auction bridge, he was recommended to the Navy's cryptographic section, heading it from 1925 to 1927, before moving on to the newly created OP-20-G. He was sent to Japan to learn the language, then moved into naval intelligence.

In 1941, he was sent to head the Combat Intelligence Unit in Hawaii, also known as 'Station Hypo'. Having failed to warn of the attack on Pearl Harbor, he dedicated himself to Anglo-American efforts to break the Japanese naval code JN-25. Though his reading of the code was far from complete, he spotted that the Japanese intended to attack Midway.

in Hawaii. Rochefort was an expert in radio communications, a cryptanalyst and a Japanese speaker. His unit was renamed the Combat Intelligence Unit. While teams in Washington, the Philippines and Singapore were working on JN-25, he attacked lesser codes concerning engineering, administration, personnel, weather and fleet exercises. A Purple machine was being made for use in Hawaii at the time. It never arrived.

In July, the Combat Intelligence Unit overheard radio traffic leading them to believe that, following the fall of France, Japan was intending to take over the French colonies in Indochina – Vietnam, Laos and Cambodia. Orders had been sent from the commander-in-chief of the Japanese fleet to the forces in the south, and it appeared that personnel had been shuffled around. Messages for certain admirals had to be

short-range transmission which would have died away before the messages reached US listening posts. American intelligence had noticed this pattern before.

Intercept messages in Red or Purple were sent by radio from US monitoring posts to Washington DC after being re-enciphered to prevent the Japanese from knowing the extent of America's interception. To cut down the traffic from the Philippines, the team did get its own Purple machine. Breaking the cipher, it only radioed back the daily keys so that cryptanalysts in Washington DC could read the messages from other monitoring stations.

As General Douglas MacArthur and Admiral Thomas C. Hart, commander-in-chief of the US Asiatic Fleet, were stationed in the Philippines, they got to see Magic too. As it was imperative the Japanese did not discover that Purple had been broken, the keys and cracked messages were sent to Washington DC using a cryptochannel called 'Copek', which used an Electric Coding Machine similar to Purple but with much stronger encryption. Traffic using Copek was kept to a minimum so as not to alert the enemy; but Rochefort was able to read Copek.

Efforts were also made to tap the phone and telegraph lines of the Japanese consulate in Hawaii. A young ensign there named Takeo Yoshikawa was sending back reports on the American ships in Pearl Harbor. On 4 December 1941, he wired Japan's foreign minister, saying: 'At 1 o'clock on the 4th a light cruiser of the Honolulu class hastily departed.' This was sent, not in the naval code, but in the diplomatic code which had already been broken.

redirected. Then there was radio silence from the fleet. It was assumed that the task force was underway. Messages were sent to it, but none were returned.

The Unit also noted that there were no messages to or from the aircraft carriers. It was assumed that these had been held behind in home waters where communication would be by low-power,

'On the so-called translator is forced the job of taking unrelated syllables and grouping them into intelligible words . . . and then going ahead with the translation, which is a much more difficult job than simple translation.'

Captain Arthur H. McCollum, Head of the Far East Section, Office of Naval Intelligence

Higher security messages used a series of transposition codes before they were enciphered in Purple. However, as the earlier transposition codes had been broken, decrypting the message was a relatively simple, though laborious task.

A sense of security

US security was anything but tight. The decrypted texts of Japanese messages, even giving the message number, were transmitted in dispatches. A Magic memorandum was found in a presidential aide's wastepaper bin

and a cipher clerk was caught trying to sell information in Boston.

On 28 April 1940, the German embassy in Washington DC reported to Berlin that

General Douglas MacArthur.

ARTHUR H. McCOLLUM (1898–1976)

As head of the Far Eastern Section of the Office of Naval Intelligence, it was Captain McCollum's job to distribute Magic, the intercepted Japanese intelligence, including Japan's effective declaration of war on the United States. A career Navy officer, McCollum had been born in Nagasaki, Japan, the son of two Baptist missionaries. After graduating from the US Naval Academy at Annapolis, Maryland, in 1921, he returned to Japan for three years of study as an interpreter and translator. He commanded a submarine and served on a battleship, and gained a special insight into the situation in the Far East as assistant naval attaché in Tokyo and an intelligence officer with the Pacific Fleet.

In October 1940, he was working with the Office of Naval Intelligence, when he produced the so-called McCollum Memo which detailed an eight-point plan to provoke Japan into war without violating the Neutrality Act signed by President Roosevelt in 1935.

the State Department had the keys to the Japanese codes. News of the breach was passed on to Tokyo. While US cryptanalysts held their breath, the Japanese Foreign ministry contacted Ambassador Kichisaburo Nomura in Washington DC, who assured them that 'the most stringent precautions were taken by all custodians of codes and ciphers'. Nevertheless, Nomura had his suspicions.

The US cryptanalysts feared that the codes would be changed and they would have to start all over again. But messages circulated by the Japanese simply gave instructions to tighten security. One of these told embassies to print *Kokka Kimitsu* – 'State Secret' – in red enamel on their cipher machines. It seems the Japanese, like the Germans, believed that their cipher was impregnable.

US security was little better. One of their greatest problems was finding a sufficient number of translators who could pass the rigorous vetting, given the misgivings surrounding Japanese–Americans at the time. Simply knowing the Japanese language was not enough. Recruits had to have at least a year's experience in telegraphic Japanese, which was a language within a language!

According to Captain Arthur H. McCollum, head of the Far East Section of the Office of Naval Intelligence, himself a Japanese-language officer: 'The so-called translator in this type of stuff almost has to be a cryptographer himself. You understand that these things come out in the form of syllables, and it is how you group your syllables that you make your words. There is no punctuation. Now, without the Chinese ideograph to read from, it is most difficult

to group these things together. That is, any two sounds grouped together to make a word may mean a variety of things. For instance, 'ba' may mean 'horses' or 'fields', 'old women', or 'my hand', all depending on the ideographs with which it is written.'

In autumn 1941, as US–Japanese relations were reaching breaking point, SIS and OP-20-G were handling up to 75 messages a day, some as long as 15 typewritten pages. On at least one occasion, 130 messages had to be decrypted in a day. As negotiations between the US and Japan continued, these would have to be cracked, translated and rushed to the Secretary of State before the Japanese ambassador arrived.

On 16 October 1941, Hideki Tojo became prime minister of Japan. One of the first things he did in office was summon the cable chief Kazuji Kameyama and ask him whether diplomatic communications were secure. 'This time,' said Kameyama, 'it's all right.'

Preparations for war

The plan for the attack on Pearl Harbor was now in place and the strike force began to gather off the remote Etoforu Island in the Kurile Islands to the north of Japan. Regular radio officers continued to send seemingly routine messages in their familiar 'fists'. The US monitoring station at Bainbridge Island in Puget Sound picked up a message

'Although I do not know which ones, I have discovered the United States is reading some of our codes.'
Ambassador Kichisaburo Nomura, 1940

instructing Japan's Washington embassy to listen to the Japanese daily news bulletin broadcast on shortwave. If they heard the phase 'east wind rain' it meant that US–Japanese relations were being broken off and they should destroy all code papers. 'North wind cloudy' meant there had been a rupture in relations with the Soviet Union, while 'west wind clear' meant the same had happened with the British. So that there would be no mistake, the phrase would be repeated in the bulletin. Once this message had been decoded by the Americans, monitoring stations turned their attention to shortwave broadcasts and translators were soon overwhelmed.

On 20 November, ambassadors Nomura and Saburo Kurusu presented an ultimatum to Secretary of State Cordell Hull. They insisted that the US abandon its support

Emperor Hirohito of Japan, delivering his message to war minister Lieutenant General Hideki Tojo, following the military ceremony held on the Yoyogi Parade Grounds, Tokyo, 21 October 1940, to mark the 2,600th anniversary of the founding of the Japanese Empire.

for China, allow the Japanese to make further conquests and provide them with as much oil as they needed. Japanese embassies elsewhere were told to conclude any business with the Americans.

The 32 ships of the strike force left the Kuriles on 25 November under strict radio silence. When Hull gave Nomura his reply countering the Japanese demands, Kurusu made a coded phone call to Tokyo, telling them that negotiations were getting nowhere. The Americans, of course, had tapped the line and the code was transparent.

The premise was that negotiations would take the form of a marriage proposal. President Roosevelt was referred to as Miss Kimiko, while the Secretary of State was Miss Fumeko. The resolution of the China question (Japan had invaded in 1937) was referred to as the imminent birth of a child. Kurusu warned that a crisis was imminent. Despite this, he was told to continue the negotiations.

More code words were circulated in case further communication had to be made in plain language. *ARIMURA*, for example, meant that enciphered communications were prohibited. *HATTORI* meant that relations had reached crisis point with a particular country. *MINAMI* was code for the USA.

To indicate where these words should be seen as code, instead of literally, telegrams containing code words should end with the English word STOP, rather than the Japanese OWARI.

A message from Ambassador Oshima in Berlin was intercepted. It told Tokyo that German Foreign Minister Joachim von Ribbentrop had assured him: 'Should Japan become engaged in a war against the United States, Germany, of course, would join the war immediately.'

Tokyo replied: 'Say very secretly to them that there is extreme danger that war may suddenly break out between the Anglo-Saxon nations and Japan through some clash of arms and add that the time of the outbreak of this war may come more quickly than anyone dreams.'

When Roosevelt read this intercept, he asked for a copy. Making copies of Magic was forbidden, but the president was allowed to keep a paraphrased version.

Changing call signs

On 1 December 1941, the Japanese Navy unexpectedly changed all its call signs. This usually happened every six months; the last call sign change had been on 1 November. The Americans realized that something was afoot, but Rochefort had to admit to his boss, the Commander-in-chief of the Pacific Fleet, Admiral Husband E. Kimmel, that he still did not know where the Japanese aircraft carriers were. The consensus was that they were still in home waters.

Meanwhile Rochefort's attempts to re-establish who the senders and receivers were became hampered by a large amount of dummy traffic and transmissions sent to multiple addressees. However, he quickly noticed that none of it was coming from the carriers or submarines. The traffic seemed to indicate an attack to the south, on Siam (Thailand) or Singapore.

Also on 1 December, OP-20-G read a Purple message from Tokyo to Washington DC reminding them of how to destroy their codes. Instructions on how to destroy their Purple machines had been given five days earlier. Another message implied that the Japanese were planning to attack British and Dutch possessions in Southeast Asia, not the USA. It said that the code machines in London, Singapore and Manila had been disposed of, while the one in Batavia (Jakarta) had been returned to Japan.

The strike force now at sea picked up a blanket broadcast to all ships, which said: 'NIITAKA-YAMA NOBORE – Climb Mount Niitaka'. It was the code to proceed with the attack.

Burn the codebooks

Back in Honolulu, a turf war had broken out with the FBI over wire taps, causing the navy to end their surveillance of the Japanese consulate, but not before they had overheard the instruction to burn all codebooks and secret documents. The following day, 3 December, SIS in Washington, DC deciphered a Purple message from Tokyo telling the embassy there to do the same. Reading the Magic decrypt, President Roosevelt concluded that war was inevitable. The only question was when would it happen?

Along with the codebooks and secret documents, the Japanese embassy in Washington, DC was told to destroy all

An Imperial Japanese Navy Air Force surveillance aircraft is loaded to an aircraft carrier circa May 1942 in Truk Islands, Micronesia. Truk Islands (now known as Chuuk Islands) was under Japanese occupation during the Pacific War.

but one of its Purple machines. First, the machines had to be dismantled with a screwdriver. Then the parts had to be hammered flat and dissolved in acid supplied by the naval attaché. In Tokyo too, the US military attaché was told to destroy war department documents.

On 4 December, monitoring stations picked up a weather forecast saying, 'north wind cloudy'. US intelligence officers were relieved there was no mention of 'east wind rain', and concluded it was not a genuine warning that Japanese–Soviet relations had broken down.

Following Hull's rejection of their ultimatum, the Japanese foreign minister met with representatives of the Imperial Army and Navy on 5 December to discuss what time they should send a detailed notification to the United States amounting to a declaration of war. It was decided that planned delivery should be postponed half-an-hour until 1 p.m. EST on 7 December, an hour after dawn in Hawaii. Vice Admiral Seiichi Itô asked Foreign Minister Shigenori Togo not to 'cable the notification to the embassy in Washington too early'.

PEARL HARBOR – COULD THE ATTACK HAVE BEEN PREVENTED?

It is clear that SIS and OP-20-G had a clear insight into the Japanese build-up for offensive action in the Pacific and they had intercepted what amounted to a declaration of war hours before the attack on Pearl Harbor. But there was no indication in the Japanese radio traffic that Pearl Harbor was the target. There were plenty of messages detailing movements in and out of Pearl Harbor, but there were similar messages concerning traffic in and out of other American ports and warships going through the Panama Canal.

The Congressional Committee investigating the attack on Pearl Harbor in 1945 made a minute-by-minute study of the actions of the codebreakers and exonerated them, instead finding that their devotion to duty 'merits the highest commendation'. The committee went on to find that, in the 1,350 days of war following the attack, the cryptanalysts 'contributed enormously to the defeat of the enemy and greatly shortened the war, and saved many thousands of lives'.

Declarations of war

Around 1 p.m. on 6 December, Japan's declaration of war arrived in the cable room of the Japanese foreign ministry. Kameyama broke the 5,000-word notification into 14 parts for ease of transmission, then had the parts enciphered on the Purple machines. He also enciphered a shorter note, warning the Washington embassy that a reply to Hull's note was on its way. The SIS had deciphered this before the Japanese had begun to send the first 13 parts of the notification. As instructed, Kameyama held back the crucial fourteenth part.

The monitoring station on Bainbridge Island picked up the first 13 parts and sent them to OP-20-G to decipher. The SIS also pitched in, but the messages were garbled and the ciphertext had to be run through the Navy's Purple machine again.

By that time, cipher clerks in the Japanese embassy were working on the notification too. The Americans had finished deciphering all 13 parts when the Japanese, after deciphering the first seven or eight parts, took a break to attend a leaving party at the Mayflower Hotel. Meanwhile, cryptographers in the State Department were encoding a personal appeal for peace from the President of the United States to the Emperor of Japan.

In Honolulu, Army counter-intelligence became concerned over a tapped phone call between a Japanese journalist and her editor in Tokyo in which the journalist said, 'the hibiscus and poinsettia are in bloom'. Surely this was code? At the same time, Takeo Yoshikawa was using an RCA connector to telegraph home details of the shipping in Pearl Harbor.

In Washington DC, the first 13 parts of the notification were being circulated as Magic. When Roosevelt read it, he said, simply: 'This means war.'

With him was Harry Hopkins, administrator of the Lend-Lease programme, who advised Roosevelt to strike the first blow.

'We can't do that,' said Roosevelt. 'We are a democracy and a peaceful people.'

Others privy to Magic that night agreed that negotiations were at an end. Everyone was on tenterhooks while awaiting the fourteenth and final part. Checks were made to see whether one of the monitoring stations had picked it up, but neglected to forward it. In fact, the Japanese Foreign Office had held it up until the last possible moment.

President Franklin Delano Roosevelt.

Finally, 14 hours after the end of the last transmission, Bainbridge Island picked up the fourteenth part. It took the Americans an hour to decipher. Like the rest of the notification, it was in English. Meantime, another message was picked up in Japanese and had to be sent to the SIS for translation. Nevertheless, they were way ahead of the cipher clerks in the Japanese embassy, who had been stood down for the night and were only recalled at 8 a.m the next morning.

When, by 4 a.m., OP-20-G had deciphered the fourteenth part, it was rushed to the White House and the State Department. By 9 a.m., the SIS had finished the translation of the second message. It instructed the Japanese embassy to deliver the 14-part notification to Secretary Hull at 1 p.m., and its meaning was clear to everyone who read it.

The notification sent the cipher clerks in the Japanese embassy into a frenzy. They had the rest of it to decipher, and only one Purple machine to do it with.

While the first wave of Japanese planes took off from aircraft carriers in the Pacific, Ambassador Nomura called Secretary Hull to request a meeting at 1 p.m. Another Japanese message had been intercepted, this one in plain language. It ended with the tell-tale 'STOP' and included the words '*HATTORI MINAMI*'. It was ordering the destruction of the last Purple machine at the Japanese embassy in Washington, D.C.

Wary of the security of telephone scramblers, the Chief of Staff George C. Marshall sent out an enciphered warning to his commanding generals in Hawaii, the Caribbean, along the West Coast and in the Philippines – the despatch to the Philippines was to be given priority.

Notification of attack

Around 12.30 p.m., Japanese embassy staff finished deciphering part 14 of the notification; but the previous 13 parts were still being typed up. The embassy then called the State Department and requested that Nomura's meeting with Hull be postponed until 1.45 p.m.

Within minutes of the call, Japanese bombers and torpedo planes were attacking the US Pacific Fleet in Pearl Harbor. At 2.05 p.m., by the time Nomura and Kurusu arrived at the State Department with the notification, Hull received a call from Roosevelt saying he had received an unconfirmed report that Pearl Harbor was under attack.

Hull invited the ambassadors into his office at 2.20 p.m. He didn't ask them to sit down. Nomura told Hull that his government had instructed him to deliver this document to him at 1 p.m., but he had been delayed because of difficulties decoding it.

In his memoirs, Hull recalled: 'I made a pretense of glancing through the note. I knew its contents already but naturally could

The inferno at Pearl Harbor, 7 December 1941.

give no indication of the fact. . . . When I finished skimming the pages, I turned to Nomura and put my eye on him.

"'I must say," I said, "that in all my conversations with you during the last nine months I have never uttered one word of untruth. This is borne out absolutely by the record. In all my fifty years of public service I have never seen a document that was more crowded with infamous falsehoods and distortions – infamous falsehoods and distortions on a scale so huge that I never imagined until today that any government on this planet was capable of uttering them."

'The ambassadors turned without a word and walked out, their heads down.'

Element of surprise

For the moment, it seemed that the Japanese attempt to maintain the element of surprise had paid off. But the commencement of hostilities without first declaring war would become part of the charges laid against Japan after the war. Some of the perpetrators, tried and convicted as war criminals, paid with their lives.

Marshall's warning arrived in Hawaii after the attack had begun. It then had to be deciphered and only reached the commanding general, Major General Walter Short, at 3 p.m. After a quick glance, he flung it straight in the bin.

Monitoring stations had already picked up a Japanese news broadcast announcing the 'death-defying raid' on Pearl Harbor. It broke off to give a weather forecast: 'West wind clear'. Within eight hours, the Japanese had also attacked the British colony of Hong Kong.

Despite their best efforts, the cryptanalysts hadn't managed to warn of the attack on Pearl Harbor; but their continued efforts to crack codes bore fruit. In the next phase of the war – the battles in the Pacific – cryptanalysis proved decisive. In April 1943, an American cryptanalyst managed to identify the itinerary for a visit to the Solomon Islands by Admiral Isoroku Yamamoto, the architect of the attack on Pearl Harbor. Eighteen P-38 fighters were sent to intercept his plane over Bougainville Island – they shot it down and he was killed.

THE FOURTEENTH PART

'Obviously it is the intention of the American Government to conspire with Great Britain and other countries to obstruct Japan's efforts toward the establishment of peace through the creation of a New Order in East Asia, and especially to preserve Anglo-American rights and interests by keeping Japan and China at war. This intention has been revealed clearly during the course of the present negotiations. Thus, the earnest hope of the Japanese Government to adjust Japanese–American relations and to preserve and promote the peace of the Pacific through cooperation with the American Government has finally been lost.

'The Japanese Government regrets to have to notify hereby the American Government that in view of the attitude of the American Government it cannot but consider that it is impossible to reach an agreement through further negotiations.'

The much-delayed Japanese declaration of war on the United States

CHAPTER 12

CRYPTOLOGY STRIKES BACK

'I can offer a lot of excuses, but we failed in our job. An intelligence officer has one job, one task, one mission – to tell his commander, his superior, today what the Japanese are going to do tomorrow.'

Lieutenant Commander Joseph J. Rochefort,
Head of the Combat Intelligence Unit in
Hawaii, December 1941

The American people were told that the surprise attack on Pearl Harbor was an 'intelligence failure'. The codebreakers in Hawaii and Washington, D.C. were determined not to take the blame for another catastrophe. Six months later, they were responsible for the victory at Midway, which turned the war in the Pacific in America's favour.

During the Battle of Midway, dive bombers from USS Hornet *approach the burning Japanese heavy cruiser* Mikuma *to make the third set of attacks on her, during the early afternoon of 6 June 1942.*

Station Hypo

The Combat Intelligence Unit in Hawaii, known as Station Hypo, had already moved from the second floor of the Administration Building into the huge basement – 18m (60ft) x 30m (100ft) – known as the Dungeon. The move was partly to accommodate extra staff (the Combat Intelligence Unit had swelled to 47), but also to keep the IBM machines, which were soon handling three million punch cards a month, cool in the tropical heat. Eventually air conditioning was installed, but it performed so erratically that station head Commander Rochefort wore a smoking jacket over his uniform to keep warm. He also wore carpet slippers to ease his feet, sore from 20-hour shifts standing on the concrete floor. His senior cryptanalyst, Lieutenant Commander Thomas H. Dyer, worked even longer shifts – up to 48 hours – thanks to the bucket of pep pills he kept on his desk.

Although it was difficult to keep up with the frequent changes in the Japanese codes, the codebreakers began to understand the underlying principles involved. Breaking JN-25 now seemed a matter of manpower. Rochefort took any Japanese speaker he could find, and even employed the band from the crippled battleship *California*. After all, his mentor Agnes Driscoll had been a musician. The number of staff at Station Hypo swelled to 120. Soon Rochefort was reading between 500 and 1,000 dispatches a day.

New codebook

On 1 April 1942, the Japanese introduced Naval Codebook D, which the Americans called JN-25c. Difficulties in distributing the new codebooks postponed its use until 1 May, giving Station Hypo more time to mine JN-25b. By 17 April, they could read enough of it to discern that the Japanese planned to seize Port Moresby in New Guinea and threaten Australia. The new Commander-in-chief of the US Pacific Fleet, Admiral Chester W. Nimitz, sent two

THOMAS H. DYER (1902–85)

After graduating from the Naval Academy in 1924, Thomas H. Dyer served as a communications officer. In 1931, he was assigned to OP-20-G where he trained under Agnes Driscoll. He then began using IBM tabulators to sort through the myriad solutions for ciphers and codes, earning himself the accolade 'the father of machine cryptanalysis'.

In 1936, he was transferred to Hawaii. His IBM machines followed him and he soon showed he could break any code or cipher more quickly with these than by hand. His machine-led attack on the JN-25 code resulted in the US victory at Midway.

In February 1946, he transferred to the Naval Security Station in Washington, D.C. After moving to the Armed Forces Security Agency in 1949, he became NSA Far East chief in Tokyo. He returned to Washington, D.C. in 1954 to become the NSA's first historian. After retiring from the US Navy the following year, he taught mathematics at the University of Maryland.

Members of the Salvage Division discuss the salvage of USS California *at Pearl Harbor, circa February–March 1942. Refloated, she took part in the invasions of the Philippines and Okinawa.*

carriers, the *Lexington* and *Yorktown* under Rear Admiral Frank Fletcher. The result was the Battle of the Coral Sea. Raging from 4 to 8 May, it was the first naval battle fought entirely by aircraft where the opposing ships could not even see one another. There were heavy losses on both sides, but the Japanese were left with too few planes to cover the landings on New Guinea and had to turn back.

While the *Yorktown* was badly damaged and the *Lexington* had to be scuttled, the battle had been a victory for the cryptanalysts, who continued working 24 hours a day. When the meaning of a code group was cracked, either by their own

---

AGNES DRISCOLL (1889–1971)

With a degree in mathematics and physics, Agnes Driscoll was also fluent in French, German, Latin and Japanese. In Amarillo, Texas, she worked as director of music at Lowry Phillips Military Academy before teaching mathematics at Amarillo High School.

In 1918, the US Navy finally allowed women to enlist and Driscoll soon found herself in the Code and Signal section of the Director of Naval Communications. After the war, she stayed on as a civilian, except for a sojourn working with Edward Hebern in his Electric Code Company, after she had shown how his cipher could be broken.

She taught Rochefort codebreaking and they worked together breaking the Red and Blue Book codes. She later made critical inroads into JN-25, but was moved on to the team working on the German Navy Enigma.

A wave breaks over the oiler Neosko, *engulfing the hose crew, as she refuels USS* Yorktown *in early May 1942, shortly before the Battle of the Coral Sea, where she was scuttled.*

efforts or by the efforts of other units sending their results via Copek, the data they revealed was punched on to IBM cards and stored in the machine.

JN-25 was super-enciphered using additive tables (see box) – numbers were added to the list of code numbers to further encrypt the message. When an intercept arrived, it was punched on to an IBM card. Then repeated subtractions were made, looking for a common remainder. A little human brainpower was needed to reconstruct the additive sequence, which was then stripped from the enciphered message. The placode (plaincode that has been deciphered from super-encipherment, but has not yet been decoded) groups could then be compared with the decodes stored on the machine. The plaintext – or as much of it as could be recovered – was then printed out. With parts not deciphered, frequency counts could be made and other statistical methods employed, for example, looking at the juxtaposition of code groups.

ADDITIVE CODES AND CIPHERS

Once a word or phrase is coded as a number – JN-25 used five digits – taken from a codebook, it can then be enciphered by adding another number, or sequence of numbers to it. Additive ciphers work by taking the digital value of a letter, given by the Baudot teleprinter code or the ASCII computer code, and adding a number or sequence of numbers to it. Additive codes and ciphers can be further enciphered using an Enigma, Purple, Red or SIGABA/ECM machine. To decrypt, the process is reversed. The ciphertext received is run back through the machine, then the agreed addition is subtracted. With an additive cipher, this gives plaintext. An additive code would then still need to be referred back to a codebook.

Traffic analysis

Not all intercepts were decrypted. Japanese traffic was too heavy and much of it was routine. By looking out for where the

> 'By Dec. 7, JN25 consisted of 50,000 code groups. And by Dec. 7, about 2,000 had been compromised, by no means enough to read any messages.'
>
> Historian Elliot Carlson on naval communications prior to Pearl Harbor

message had come from, who it was directed to and how long it was, traffic analysts who sifted through Japanese communications day in, day out got a feel for which messages were important. If they were unsure, the message was sampled by partially decrypting it. Those deemed important enough were translated, written up and passed to Nimitz's chief of staff, who then decided which ones should be shown to the admiral.

At the beginning of May 1942, the wireless traffic changed. The sheer volume indicated that the Japanese were planning something. Fortunately, the implementation of JN-25c was delayed a further month. By then, Station Hypo had constructed around a third of JN-25b's codebook and could read about 90 per cent of the intercepts.

Midway

On 14 May 1942, Rochefort came across the words *koryaku butai* – invasion force – in an intercept. It was followed by the location AF. Another message ordered airbase equipment to be sent to Saipan ready for use by 'AF ground crews'. So AF was an airbase – Rochefort reasoned that it had to be Midway.

Reading between the lines, it seemed that after a diversionary attack on the Aleutians, Yamamoto aimed to lure the remains of the Pacific Fleet to Midway where he intended to destroy it. Nimitz realized that if he could get to Midway first he could turn the tables on the Japanese. But he had to be sure; otherwise he would be leaving Hawaii undefended.

Admiral Isoroku Yamamoto.

OP-20-G in Washington, DC claimed that Station Hypo had got their additive tables wrong. It was not AF, they said, but AG – Johnson Island. Others thought the whole thing a deceptive ploy and believed the real target to be the West Coast of the United States. The situation seemed even more fishy when they intercepted a message from a Japanese seaplane unit informing the Personnel Bureau in Tokyo that their new address was going to be Midway Island. General Marshall said they were laying it on a bit too thick for the intelligence to be believed.

But Rochefort came up with a plan to prove he was right. The Midway garrison should report that the desalination plant on

the island had broken down. The message was bound to be picked up by the Japanese. Two days later, a US monitoring station intercepted a JN-25 message reporting that AF was low on fresh water, and confirming that AF was Midway. To maintain the fiction, Hawaii sent a message, saying that supplies of fresh water were on their way.

On 27 May 1942, Rochefort incurred the displeasure of senior staff officers when he turned up late for a meeting. He had been up all night breaking a crucial piece of JN-25b, a code within a code used for dates. An earlier decrypt had shown that the air assault on the island would come from the west. He had now discovered that it would begin on 3 June. Again, this was an extraordinary stroke of luck. That same day, 27 May, the Japanese switched codebooks and additive tables, and imposed a radio blackout on the task force.

Nimitz sent the aircraft carriers USS *Enterprise*, *Hornet* and the rapidly repaired *Yorktown*. On 2 June, they were stationed 560km (350 miles) northeast of Midway. Meanwhile, a force of cruisers and destroyers was sent northwards to the Aleutians to

The scene on board USS Yorktown, *shortly after she had been hit by three Japanese bombs on 4 June 1942.*

protect the flank. The Americans had the advantage that they had land-based planes on Midway and also on Hawaii, which was within range. The Japanese had no land-based support for their carrier force.

The battle began on 3 June, when US bombers from Midway attacked the Japanese carriers when they were still 350km (220 miles) southwest of the American fleet. The ensuing battle raged for four days. The US Navy lost the *Yorktown*, but the Japanese Imperial Navy fared far worse, losing four of the large aircraft carriers that had led the attack on Pearl Harbor. The Japanese advance in the Pacific was halted. After the cryptographic triumph at Midway, there would be nothing but retreat for Japan.

When the battle was over, Rochefort told his staff he did not want to see them for three or four days, expecting them to go home and sleep. Instead they had a drunken house party lasting three days on Diamond Head. Then they returned, with hangovers, to resume long shifts trying to decrypt JN-25c, then JN-25d which was introduced in August.

Nimitz recommended Rochefort for the Distinguished Service Medal, but Rochefort advised against it, saying it would only make trouble as OP-20-G in Washington, DC were trying to claim credit for breaking the codes that had given the USA victory at Midway.

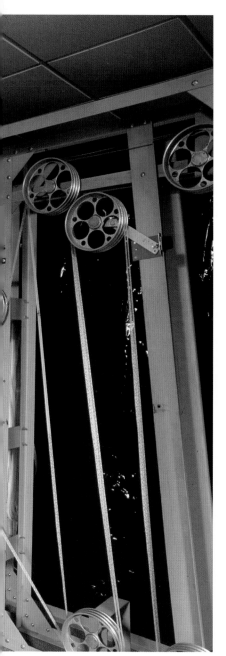

CHAPTER 13

COMPUTER CRYPTANALYSIS

'I do not imagine that any war since classical times, if ever, has been fought in which one side read consistently the main military and naval intelligence of the other. Of course, the Germans read a fair amount of our own codes, but in nothing like the comprehensive and all-embracing manner in which we read theirs.'

Stuart Milner-Barry,
Hut 6, Bletchley Park

Breaking Enigma had given victory in the Battle of Britain, at el-Alamein and in the Battle of the Atlantic. But if the war was to be won, the battle had to be taken to the enemy. To do that, the codebreakers at Bletchley Park had to crack the far more secure cipher produced by the German high command's sophisticated Lorenz machines.

A recreation of the Colossus codebreaking computer at Bletchley Park.

'Tunny'

Before Turing left for the USA in November 1942, he moved from Hut 8 to Bletchley Park's Research Centre where work was being done on traffic emanating from the new German Lorenz cipher machines. The British gave the Lorenz machine the codename 'Tunny'. While the Enigma machine produced ciphertext which was handed to a radio operator to transmit in Morse code by hand, the Lorenz machine did the process in one go. The operator simply typed in the message, or used paper tape with the message punched into it, and the machine enciphered it, then transmitted it in the standard five-bit Baudot code. At the receiving station, the transmission was deciphered by another Lorenz machine and printed out. The Germans were so confident that the Lorenz system was secure, they sent everything in plaintext, without encoding messages first.

When a key was pressed on the Lorenz machine, the letter was encoded digitally. Inside the machine were 12 wheels that generated a stream of seemingly random numbers which were added to the message code. At the receiving end, the Lorenz machine was set up in the same way to generate an identical stream of random numbers. These were subtracted from the enciphered transmission, leaving the original message clear.

At Bletchley Park, cryptanalyst Brigadier John Tiltman immediately spotted a flaw in the Lorenz cipher. It used the Vernam system (see page 87), which was well known in codebreaking circles. Tiltman reasoned that if two messages were encoded using the same key to set up the machine (given at the beginning of each message) then the two messages could simply be added together, and the random numbers generated by the Lorenz

The Lorenz cipher machine.

machine would cancel out, leaving the two messages blended together. Using intelligent guesswork, Tiltman found that it was possible to work out sections of the messages.

A terrible mistake

The radio interception station at Knockholt in Kent began to collect a number of these messages with the same indicator. They were called 'depths'. Then the Germans made a terrible mistake. An operator was sending a long message of some 4,000 characters from Athens to Vienna; the operator at the receiving end replied that there was some problem and asked him to send the message

> 'It was around this time . . . that Max made his first breakthrough – the idea of mechanizing Tutte's method using high-speed electronic counters.'
>
> Cryptographer Max Newman's son, William, speaking about his father's work on Tunny

again. Against all regulations, the operator sent the message a second time using the same settings. If he had sent exactly the same text again the second time, adding the two messages together would have cancelled the whole thing out.

JOHN TILTMAN (1894–1982)

Serving in France in World War I, John Tiltman was severely wounded on the Somme. After the war he was attached to a small signal intelligence organization in London, before being posted to Simla in India where he spent eight years codebreaking.

In the 1930s he led a team breaking Comintern codes, showing that the Communist Party of Great Britain was dependent on support from Moscow. Running training courses in Bedford, he earmarked recruits for signals intelligence work. By 1939, he was head of the military section at Bletchley Park, where he rose to become chief cryptographer.

In February 1941, he broke the German railway Enigma that revealed their preparations for attacks on Greece and the Soviet Union. He learned enough Japanese to collaborate with the Americans in breaking the JN-25 naval code. After the war, he stayed on with GCHQ. When he retired, he moved to Washington, DC, where he became a consultant to the National Security Agency.

The ciphertext was sent to Tiltman, who discovered that the first message started with SPRUCHNUMMER, 'message number', while in the second this was abbreviated to SPRUCHNR. The slight difference between the two allowed Tiltman to decipher the plaintext of both messages. Not only that, but by adding the message to the ciphertext he could work out the obscuring numbers generated by the Lorenz machine.

Tiltman gave his findings to a chemistry graduate named Bill Tutte (see box opposite). The first thing to strike Tutte was that as the indicator was 12 letters long, the Lorenz cipher must have been generated by 12 wheels. He began looking for repetitions. The first he found was a 41; he found others at 31, 29, 26 and 23; then he spotted further patterns at 43, 47, 51, 53 and 59. By isolating these, he realized that there were two streams of numbers being added together to produce the key. Without even seeing a Lorenz machine, he had discovered exactly how it worked.

The 12 wheels had pins round the circumference. These were set by the operator either to be active or inactive; active pins made a connection, giving an impulse or a 1. Inactive pins gave no impulse, making a space or a zero. The number of the pins gave the length of the pseudo-random pattern.

The first five wheels, called 'chi-wheels', had pin-lengths of 41, 31, 29, 26 and 23. They moved regularly and produced the chi-stream. The next five wheels, the 'psi-wheels', had pin-lengths of 43, 47, 51, 53 and 59. They moved when there was an impulse or 1 and stood still when there was

no impulse or a 0, producing the psi-stream.

There were two further wheels, the motor wheels, with pin-lengths of 61 and 37. The longer one moved regularly; the shorter one moved one place when there was an impulse and stayed still when there was none. All this was deduced from the transmissions themselves. No attempt was made to steal a Lorenz machine, as that may have prompted the Germans to come up with something even more complicated. So no one at Bletchley Park saw a Lorenz machine until the end of the war.

Knowing how the machine worked and breaking the code were two different things. But adding the chi- and psi- streams together to make the key and adding the key to the message to make the ciphertext was a purely mathematical process, so it was theoretically possible to break the code using mathematical means.

The intercept control room in Hut 6 at Bletchley Park. In May 1940, John Jeffreys became ill and Gordon Welchman took over as head of the hut. Stuart Milner-Barry succeeded Welchman when he became Assistant Director of Mechanization in the autumn of 1943.

Although Bill Tutte gained a first in chemistry at Cambridge, his passion was mathematics. In 1940, he was conscripted and after initial training sent to Bletchley Park and put to work on Tunny. Simply from the intercepts, he managed to make a virtual reconstruction of the extremely complex Lorenz machine.

At the end of the war, Tutte returned to Trinity College, Cambridge, as a research student, producing a PhD thesis on the algebraic theory of graphs. In 1948, he took a post at the University of Toronto where he continued to come up with new mathematical ideas. The Tutte polynomial was named after him.

In 1962, he moved to the newly established

University of Waterloo in Ontario. Although he retired in 1985, he continued to work in mathematics. In a lecture in 1999, he explained how his time at Bletchley Park had informed his later work.

Differencing

By the summer of 1942, Alan Turing, already something of a legend at Bletchley Park, was assigned to the Tunny task. Using a pencil, a piece of paper and an eraser, he used a process called differencing – that is, XORing one character with the next. XOR is a Boolean operator, and works like this:

$$1 + 0 = 1$$
$$0 + 1 = 1$$
$$1 + 1 = 0$$
$$0 + 0 = 0$$

Turing worked out that, on average, half the time XORing a psi character gave a null or 00000. When this was added to the chi character, it did not change it. So half the time, the key was the chi character.

Turing drew up sheets, one for each of the chi-wheels. The possible settings of the wheels were written out in columns. He then employed an iterative process, making certain guesses. When these produced inconsistencies, they were abandoned; when they did not, they were kept. This way, the settings of the chi-wheels could be deduced. Then it was possible to go back and work out the settings of the psi-wheels and the motor wheels, giving the key.

This method, known as 'Turingery' or 'Turingismus', allowed Bletchley Park to read top-secret orders signed by Hitler himself. In 1943, during the Battle of Kursk, decoded Tunny messages were sent to the Russians describing the deployment of every German division and unit. The Red Army won the battle decisively and advanced, almost unchecked, to Berlin. Even so, the Soviets didn't realize the British had broken the code and, after the war, used captured Lorenz machines themselves, imagining them to be secure.

The Testery

Meanwhile there was the wartime problem of handling large amounts of cipher traffic.

> 'I was greeted with news of instructions from the War Office that I was required for special intelligence work and that I was to proceed . . . to an unspecified "course" at Bedford. I was destined for cryptography at Bletchley Park. . . . Those on the Bedford course gave the impression of having been incongruously gathered from the hedgerows.'
>
> Roy (later Lord) Jenkins, *A Life at the Centre*, 1991

This was done by a group known as the Testery, set up in July 1942 under Major Ralph Tester. Max Newman, Turing's tutor at Cambridge, was called in to help. He thought the job could be done with the help of rapid, special-purpose electronic machinery employing paper tape and photoelectric cells.

Two long loops of teleprinter tape were prepared. One carried the ciphertext added to itself with a displacement of one. The other had all possible starting positions of chi-wheels added to themselves with a displacement of one. The two tapes were compared by the machine, character by

As the codebreaking operation at Bletchley Park expanded, more women were brought in, largely to do clerical work. However, among their number were a number of gifted mathematicians and cryptanalysts who made an enormous contribution to codebreaking.

character, and the coincidences counted. The correct settings of the chi-wheels delivered the most hits between the two tapes. The machine was called 'Heath Robinson', after the British cartoonist who drew ridiculously complex machines to perform absurdly simple tasks. The American equivalent was called 'Rube Goldberg', after an American cartoonist who also drew complicated gadgets.

It was found that paper tape could be run through the machine at up to 48kph (30mph). The chi-wheel tape tended to stretch after it had been used numerous times, rendering it useless. Synchronization between the two tapes was vital. Turing suggested they call in Tommy Flowers from the Post Office Research Station.

TOMMY FLOWERS (1905–98)

Born in the East End of London, Tommy Flowers got a scholarship to study at a technical college. At 16 he began a mechanical apprenticeship at the Royal Arsenal in Woolwich, while attending evening classes to take a degree in engineering. In 1926, he joined the Post Office as an electrical engineer and moved to the laboratories in Dollis Hill four years later. There, as early as 1934, he built experimental equipment that used over 3,000 valves.

After Flowers had delivered the prototype Colossus Mark I, it proved so reliable that he continued in production. There were ten Colossuses in operation by the end of the war. He then pioneered subscriber trunk dialling, or STD, and helped build the National Physical Laboratory's stored-program computer ACE. He also designed ERNIE, the electronic random-number generator that picked Premium Bond winners.

Colossus in action at Bletchley Park. The bigwigs thought it would not work, but Post Office engineer Tommy Flowers built it anyway and proved them wrong.

Flowers, who had worked with Turing on the bombes, suggested the job could be done with an electronic machine using over 1,000 values. This was dismissed as impractical because the heated filaments found in radio sets were apt to blow. Flowers knew this was because a radio was regularly switched on and off, so the filament was always heating up and cooling down. But if you kept the valve running all the time on a low current, the filaments rarely burnt out.

Colossus

Although his proposal had been rejected, Flowers set to work with his team at his laboratory in Dollis Hill, northwest London. In ten months he produced the first large-scale digital computer, the prototype Colossus Mark I, using 1,500 valves. In January 1944, racks of components were delivered to Bletchley Park from Flowers' laboratories, and assembled. The machine was the size of a small room and weighed about a ton.

Colossus dispensed with the chi-tape, instead storing the wheel patterns electronically. The tape carrying the ciphertext could run at up to 85kph (53mph) before it broke; 43.9kph (27.3mph) was settled on, allowing the machine to read 5,000 characters a second.

A full-scale version, the Colossus Mark II featuring 2,500 valves, was ready by D-Day. Using five tape channels, this was five times faster than the prototype. It was thought to have tipped the balance of the war in the Allies' favour. Reading 25,000 characters a second, it was comparable with the first Intel microprocessor chip introduced 30 years later.

After the war, two machines were retained by GCHQ. The rest were broken up, though parts were taken to the newly created Computer Machine Laboratory at Manchester University. As those who knew about Colossus were bound by the Official Secrets Act, it was never spoken of; for years it was believed that ENIAC (the Electronic Numerical Integrator and Computer) built at the University of Pennsylvania, was the first large-scale electronic computer.

While Turing has been credited with the building of Colossus, he had little to do with it. Flowers had read Turing's 1936 paper on the theoretical Universal Machine, but Tommy was a practical man and did not understand much of it. After the end of the war in Europe, Flowers and Turing visited Germany where an engineer proudly showed them a Lorenz machine, assuring them that its output was 'absolutely safe'. The two men did not let on that they were already familiar with its workings and had broken its code some years earlier.

Flowers and Turing took a special interest in the Germans' codebreaking facilities. The German Navy's B-Dienst (*Beobachtungsdienst* or surveillance service) had broken some Royal Navy ciphers, which kept U-boats informed of convoy positions, but they simply hadn't put the same effort into codebreaking as the British at Bletchley Park. Besides, many of the brightest intellects employed by the British were homosexuals or Jews; in Germany, these persecuted minorities had either fled or found themselves in death camps.

ULTRA AT D-DAY

Colossus was vital to the success of Operation Overlord, the Allied landing on the Normandy beaches on D-Day, 6 June 1944. According to Sir Harry Hinsley, official historian of British intelligence during World War II: 'As Ultra accumulated, it administered some unpleasant shocks. In particular, it revealed in the second half of May – following earlier disturbing indications that the Germans were concluding that the area between Le Havre and Cherbourg was a likely, and perhaps even the main, invasion area – that they were sending reinforcements to Normandy and the Cherbourg peninsula.' Ultra created a state of mind which transformed the taking of decisions. An American report stated that: 'To feel that you know your enemy is a vastly comforting feeling. . . . Knowledge of this kind makes your own planning less tentative and more assured, less harrowing and more buoyant.'

CHAPTER 14

COLD WAR CRYPTOGRAPHY

*'If you control the code, you control the world.
This is the future that awaits us.'*

Marc Goodman
*Future Crimes: Everything Is Connected,
Everyone Is Vulnerable and What We Can Do
About It,* 2015

The Cold War was conducted largely by spies. They needed invisible ink, one-time pads, dead-letter drops, microdots and messages sent by radio in short, high-speed bursts. But still there were codes to break and ciphers to decrypt.

RAF Fylingdales is a British Royal Air Force station high on Snod Hill in the North York Moors, England. This early attack warning Cold War facility consisted of three 40-metre-diameter 'golfballs' or geodesic domes (radomes) containing mechanically steered radar.

Spy rings

Although Britain and the USA were wartime allies of the Soviet Union, espionage continued between them throughout World War II. Afterwards, the USA and the UK remained allies, particularly in intelligence matters. With the beginning of the Cold War, the USSR became a palpable enemy, running extensive spy rings in the West. Its agents used one-time pads whose keys were kept in safes in their embassies so their codes proved impossible to break.

The pads carried by agents were tiny and easily concealed. Rudolf Ivanovich Abel, a British-born Soviet intelligence officer posing as an artist in New York, kept one the size of a postage stamp. When he was arrested in 1957, it was found inside a hollowed-out block of wood, wrapped with sandpaper like a sanding block, which had been carelessly tossed in a wastepaper bin.

Messages could also be transmitted in high-speed bursts, which meant they were difficult to detect, even by constantly scanning the radio spectrum. On the ground, messages were passed between agents and their handlers in pre-arranged 'drops'. Abel seldom met his lieutenant Reino Hayhanen, and communicated via coded messages left in hiding places such as a crack in a wall on Jerome Avenue in the Bronx, behind a brick under a bridge in Central Park or in a hole in some steps at Prospect Park, Brooklyn.

Microfilm

Messages were often reduced photographically to make them easier to conceal. Abel used 'soft' microfilm, which was made by dissolving the stiff base, leaving only the emulsion carrying the image. This could be squeezed into tiny places, such as hollowed-out pencils, bolts, torch batteries or coins, which would invite no suspicion even if found.

In the summer of 1953, newsboy James Bozart dropped a nickel. It fell apart, revealing a tiny photograph showing a series of numbers. Bozart told a friend who was the daughter of a New York cop; through him, word got back to the FBI, who enlarged the image. It showed ten columns of numbers, each five digits long; there were 21 numbers in most columns. Once the FBI had established that it was not a trick coin made for use by a magician, they tried to break the code – and failed. All they could do was establish that the numbers had been typed up on a foreign-made typewriter.

May 1963: a Sanyo portable transistor radio, Minox cameras, film and codebooks used by the British and American intelligence services.

Glienicke Bridge in Berlin was where spies were exchanged during the Cold War.

The mystery was solved four years later when Abel grew tired of Hayhanen's habit of spending the money he had been given to run a spy ring on drink and prostitutes, and had him recalled to Moscow. Fearing that he would be imprisoned or killed, Hayhanen handed himself in to the US Embassy in Paris.

When the FBI searched the modest home Hayhanen shared with his wife in Peekskill, New York, they found a 50 Markka coin from Finland which had been hollowed out. Hayhanen was questioned about the cryptosystems he had been taught to use and the FBI finally managed to decrypt the message in the nickel. It read:

'1. WE CONGRATULATE YOU ON A SAFE ARRIVAL. WE CONFIRM THE RECEIPT OF YOUR LETTER TO THE ADDRESS "V REPEAT V" AND THE READING OF LETTER NUMBER 1.

'2. FOR ORGANIZATION OF COVER, WE GAVE INSTRUCTIONS TO TRANSMIT TO YOU THREE THOUSAND IN LOCAL (CURRENCY). CONSULT WITH US PRIOR TO INVESTING IT IN ANY KIND OF BUSINESS, ADVISING THE CHARACTER OF THIS BUSINESS.

'3. ACCORDING TO YOUR REQUEST, WE WILL TRANSMIT THE FORMULA FOR THE PREPARATION OF SOFT FILM AND NEWS SEPARATELY, TOGETHER WITH (YOUR) MOTHER'S LETTER.

'4. IT IS TOO EARLY TO SEND YOU THE GAMMAS. ENCIPHER SHORT LETTERS, BUT THE LONGER ONES MAKE WITH INSERTIONS. ALL THE DATA ABOUT YOURSELF, PLACE OF WORK, ADDRESS, ETC., MUST NOT BE TRANSMITTED IN ONE CIPHER MESSAGE. TRANSMIT INSERTIONS SEPARATELY.

'5. THE PACKAGE WAS DELIVERED TO YOUR WIFE PERSONALLY. EVERYTHING IS ALL RIGHT WITH THE FAMILY. WE WISH YOU SUCCESS. GREETINGS FROM THE COMRADES. NUMBER 1, 3RD OF DECEMBER.'

The message had been sent from the Soviet Union, intended for Hayhanen, shortly after he arrived in the USA. Hayhanen then identified Abel, who was convicted of spying and sentenced to 30 years. In February 1962, Abel was exchanged for

Soviet spy Rudolf Abel was arrested in Brooklyn, New York, in 1957. He was found in possession of one-time pads.

Gary Powers, the pilot of a U-2 spy plane shot down over the Soviet Union.

Snowfall

The cipher that had confounded the FBI codebreakers was a complex one. First the plaintext was cut in half, with the second half put before the first. That buried the vulnerable beginning, which was marked in the text with a special indicator. The letters were substituted with numbers filled in on a straddling checkerboard, using the first seven letters of the word *snegopad* – 'snowfall'.

The resulting text was written horizontally into a block and the columns transposed. It was then transcribed vertically and written horizontally into a second, stepped transposition block. Each row was started one column to the right until it resulted in an empty line. The next row began under the key number 2 and at the

---

STRADDLING CHECKERBOARD

Devised in the 16th century, the straddling checkerboard was used by communists during the Spanish Civil War. It used a table and a keyword – here, FRANCO. The rest of the letters of the alphabet are filled in on the two lines below.

	0	9	8	7	6	5	4	3	2	1
	F	R	A	N	C	O				
1	B	D	E	G	H	IJ	K	L	M	P
2	Q	R	S	T	U	V	W	X	Y	Z

To encode 'attack at dawn', you take the one-digit identifier of any of the letters of the keyword, and the two-digit identifier – row, then column – of any other letter. This gives 8 27 27 8 6 14 8 27 19 8 24 7. These can then be run together as 827278614827198247 to further mystify the cryptanalyst. When the recipient who has the key comes to decode it, they can see that a 1 or a 2 should be combined with the number that follows it to give a letter, while single numbers without a 1 or 2 in front of them come from the keyword.

> 'While I cannot take the time to name all the men in the State Department who have been named as members of the Communist Party and members of a spy ring, I have here in my hand a list of 205.'
>
> Senator Joseph McCarthy's speech to members of a Women's Republican Club in 1950 illustrates the anxiety which swept America during the Cold War

left-hand side again, with each subsequent row starting one column to the right, and so on. The final ciphertext was transcribed vertically, ignoring the empty spaces caused by the stepping.

The advantage of this was that it did away with one-time pads which, like Abel's, could be found. All Hayhanen had to do was remember the Russian word for snowfall, the date Russia marked as the end of the war with Japan – 3/9/1945 – and his personal key number, which was 13 (though changed to 20 in 1956). These keys specified the transpositions and dimensions of the blocks. Though the system was complex and seemingly impossible to break, it was easy to use.

To make it even more unbreakable, an arbitrary five-digit number was added at the beginning of the key derivation. It was placed in a specified position in the ciphertext for the recipient to decode. In Hayhanen's case, it was the fifth cipher group from the end, given by the final 5 in 3/9/1945. It was changed from message to message, so every solution had to come from one message alone. Consequently, the cryptanalyst would have to try every possibility before cracking it. The nickel message had 1,035 digits, so

the odds against coming up with the right one were astronomical. In theory, this code is not unbreakable, but in practice it is. No wonder the FBI failed.

Trigonometric code

While the KGB was expert at maintaining communication security, local communist spy rings were not. On 16 August 1954, the Iranian security police arrested Ali Abbasi, a former army captain who had resigned eight years earlier in protest at corruption in the armed forces. He was by this point a prominent member of the Iranian Communist Party, Red Tudeh. A suitcase he was carrying was found to contain detailed plans of the guards' schedule at the Shah's summer palace and other papers in three codes. Two of the codes were cracked, but the third appeared to be pages of trigonometric functions, though the equations were meaningless.

Under interrogation, Abbasi said the code could only be broken by its inventor. Meanwhile the police had picked up Colonel Jamsheed Mobasheri, an artillery officer regarded by fellow officers as a mathematical genius. In the cells, Mobasheri ripped a rusty nail from the wall and tried to tear open an artery. He survived, but stubbornly insisted that his code could not be broken. But when he was visited by one of the analysts trying to break it, he could not conceal his pride in his work and indicated that the codebreaker was working along the right lines.

The cipher was broken and revealed a list of names of conspirators in the military and security forces. Four hundred were arrested; 26 – including Mobasheri – were executed.

CHAPTER 15

COMPUTERS TAKE OVER

'Cyber attacks are not what makes the cool war "cool". As a strategic matter, they do not differ fundamentally from older tools of espionage and sabotage.'

Noah Feldman
Cool War, 2013

The days when classically educated chess champions and crossword puzzle experts could sit down with pencil and paper and crack codes were long gone. Computers now went head-to-head, one creating ciphers, the other cracking them. The race was on to create the uncrackable code. This terrified the government agencies who wanted to spy on criminals and terrorists.

Modern spying is carried out using microchips and computers. The geeks have taken over from the gun-toting James Bonds.

Different world, same secrets

The development of programmable computers such as Colossus and ENIAC had moved cryptology into a different realm. Codebreakers could now check all possible keys until the right one was found. But computers aided cryptographers, too, who simply used them to build ever more complex codes. Programs could be written for virtual rotors spinning clockwise and anti-clockwise, slower and faster, in seemingly arbitrary steps. And, of course, computers could operate much faster than any mechanical system.

Even today, the basic tools of encryption (substitution and transposition) still apply and can be extended into the letters themselves. On a digital computer, letters, numbers, punctuation marks and other symbols are encoded as numbers, using various protocols. The most common is ASCII, where 128 basic characters are represented as a 7-bit set of binary codes. An extended 8-bit form of ASCII provides 256 characters that include less common symbols, accents, and so on.

The Mona Lisa stylized as ASCII artwork.

To encrypt the word AGENT, for example, the computer would first translate into binary form. In ASCII, that gives:

01000001 01000111 01000101
01001110 01010100

A simple way of enciphering it would be to take the digits in pairs and swap them round.

Plaintext: 01000001 01000111
01000101 01001110 01010100
Ciphertext: 10000010 10001011
10001010 10001101 10101000

To decipher this, it would simply be a matter of swapping the pairs of digits round again. Another way of encrypting would be to take an additive key, the name NIGEL, for instance:

Plaintext: 01000001 01000111
01000101 01001110 01010100
Key (Nigel): 01001110 01001001
01000111 01000101 01001100
Ciphertext: 010001111 010010000
010001100 010010011 010100000

Again, it is a simple matter to decode. You subtract NIGEL in binary from the ciphertext to get back to the plaintext. For anyone trying to decrypt an intercept, it is more difficult. There are no spaces, so the ciphertext is just a stream of 1s and 0s, not broken up into convenient cipher groups. The cryptanalyst would not even know if the plaintext or key was encoded in ASCII.

Lucifer

With the spread of commercial computers in the 1960s, businesses found that they needed secure communication, so a system of standardized encryption was required. The first was 'Lucifer', the brainchild of Horst Feistel, who worked with Don Coppersmith at IBM. They pioneered 'block ciphers', in which a binary stream of plaintext was split into blocks of 64 digits that were encrypted individually.

Each block was split in two. Half of it was passed through a scrambler function and added to the other half. The block was then recombined and the process repeated. This was performed numerous times before transmission. Deciphering was done by reversing the procedure. There was a choice of scrambler functions which had to be agreed between sender and recipient. Once that was fixed, the sender just had to input a key number and the message.

When IBM put Lucifer forward to the National Bureau of Standards, the NSA stepped in. Their contribution was not to make the encryption stronger, but weaker. They did not want an encryption system they could not break to be made commercially available. The key was limited to 56 bits (around 100,000,000,000,000 digits in decimal). At that time, no commercial company had the computing power to check every possible key; only the NSA had this resource. Lucifer was adopted as the Date Encryption Standard (DES) in 1976.

HORST FEISTEL (1915–90)

Born in Berlin, Horst Feistel emigrated to the USA in 1934. When Germany declared war on the USA in 1941, Feistel found himself under house arrest. However, he got his US citizenship in 1944 and went to work at the Air Force Cambridge Research Center. He moved on to MIT's Lincoln Laboratory and the MITRE Corporation, but his work on ciphers was dogged by the newly formed NSA. He developed Lucifer at IBM's Thomas J. Watson Research Center near New York. With modifications provided by the NSA, this was adopted as the Data Encryption Standard by the National Bureau of Standards.

Thomas J. Watson Research Center.

Key distribution

DES had another problem, one which had plagued codemakers down the centuries – key distribution (the process whereby the recipient of an encrypted message gets the key to decrypt it). Two companies running DES software could only communicate securely if they both had the same key, but sending this key electronically compromised security. There was no point in DES if the key could be intercepted; DES was therefore only as strong as the encryption of the key.

The only secure way to distribute the key was by courier. Messengers would fly around the world with DES cipher keys locked in briefcases chained to their wrists. For the US military, particularly, this became a huge problem. Shiploads of keys had to be exchanged. The people who addressed this problem were Whitfield Diffie, Martin Hellman and Ralph Merkle. They developed a method whereby a secret key could be shared over an insecure channel. With the growth of the internet, this became vital.

MARTIN HELLMAN (1945–)

Graduating from the Bronx High School of Science, Martin Hellman gained a degree in electrical engineering from New York University, getting his masters and a PhD at Stanford. In 1968, he worked at IBM's Thomas J. Watson Research Center where he met Horst Feistel. Then he moved on to MIT, before returning to Stanford's Electrical Engineering faculty, where Diffie caught him up. In 1976, they published *New Directions in Cryptography*, which outlined the Diffie–Hellman key exchange – though Hellman thought that Ralph Merkle should be acknowledged.

Hellman and Diffie were awarded a Marconi Fellowship in 2000 and the Turing Award in 2015. Merkle's contribution was recognized by an Association of Computer Machinery Award in 1996.

Martin Hellman and Whitfield Diffie.

The problem of the secure distribution of keys by courier was overcome by mathematicians.

The key-exchange is generally explained using three fictional characters – Alice and Bob, who want to exchange messages, and Eve, an eavesdropper. To keep her messages to Bob secure, Alice must use a different key each time. Her problem is that she has to get the keys to Bob without Eve getting hold of them, as she is eavesdropping on the line. One way is for Alice and Bob to meet and exchange keys by hand, which is inconvenient. Another is to send the keys by courier, which is expensive and carries its own risks. Messengers can be bribed, blackmailed or robbed.

Double lock

There is a way round this. The keys could be exchanged by parcel post using a simple procedure – even if the mail system is so corrupt that all unprotected correspondence is read. Alice puts the keys inside a metal box and secures it with a padlock. She then mails the box to Bob, who is unable to open it because he does not have the key. Instead, he puts his own padlock on the box and sends it back to Alice. With the key she has retained, Alice opens her padlock and mails it back to Bob. The box is still secure because it has Bob's lock on it. When Bob receives it, he uses his own key to open the box and read the cipher keys inside it.

Translating the analogy into cryptography: Alice enciphers the message with her key and sends it via the internet to Bob. It does not matter if Eve intercepts it, provided the encryption is strong enough. Bob does not have the cipher key to decrypt it, so he re-encrypts it using his own cipher key and sends it back to Alice. She then decrypts her encipherment and sends the result back to Bob, who then decrypts the message with his key and reads it.

Clearly this does not ordinarily work: to reconstitute the original message, you would have to decrypt the ciphertext using Bob's key first, not Alice's. The other way round is likely to produce gobbledegook.

One-way function

Diffie, Hellman and Merkle had seemingly run into a brick wall. But they were not deterred; they were mathematicians and knew that there must be a way around the problem. It came in the form of a one-way function.

Most mathematical functions are two-way. If you add 2 and 2, you get 4; and if you take 2 away from 4, you get back to 2. If you double 3 you get 6; halve 6 and you get back to 3. The analogy is with a light switch: flick it one way and the light comes on; flick it back the other way and the light goes off again, returning to its original state.

One-way functions are those that are not reversible. The analogy here is with mixing paint. Adding one colour to another is easy; separating them again to give the two original colours is all but impossible. Similarly with an egg – once cracked, it can't be uncracked. In mathematics, these one-way functions are sometimes called 'Humpty Dumpty' functions.

Modular arithmetic is full of one-way functions. It is also known as clock arithmetic. Think of the face of a standard 12-hour clock. If it is ten o'clock and you add three hours, you get to one o'clock. Arithmetically, this is written as: 10 + 3 = 1 (mod 12).

The same thing works with angles. Add 180 degrees to 270 and you complete one revolution of 360 degrees, then move on to 90: 270 + 180 = 90 (mod 360). But any modulus can be used: 6 + 3 = 2 (mod 7).

The easiest way to do modular arithmetic is to work out the answer in standard arithmetic and divide it by the modulus; the answer in modular arithmetic is the remainder.

Consider the function 5^x (x indicates the number of times 5 is multiplied by itself). If $x = 2$, then 5^x (or 5 x 5) = 25. So the function turns 5 into 25. It is a two-way function. Given the answer, you could work backwards and deduce that the original number was 2. Even by guessing, you can easily arrive at the right answer. Say the answer is 125 and you guess, wrongly, that the original number is 4. By doing the maths (5^4 or 5 x 5 x 5 x 5 = 625) you realize your guess is too big. You have already established that 2 is too small, so you try 3 – 5^3 (5 x 5 x 5) = 125 – which is correct.

But it does not work out that way in modular arithmetic. Take the function 5^x (mod 7).

x	2	3	4	5	6	7	8	9
5^x (mod 7)	4	6	2	3	1	5	4	6

It is not possible to work backwards easily from the answer to the original number without trying them all one by one. But say the function was 297^x (mod 4,283) and the answer was 402? If I know the value of x, this takes seconds to work out, but

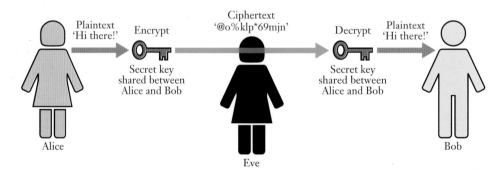

Symmetric encryption: Alice sends a message to Bob using their shared key. Eve can see the ciphertext, but can't see the plaintext because she doesn't have the key. Bob uses the shared key to decipher the message.

working backwards it takes hours of tedious calculation to discover that x is 546. And, of course, computers can deal with much larger numbers than these.

Say Alice and Bob talk on the phone and agree that y = 5 and z = 7 in the function y^x (mod z). It does not matter if Eve is listening in because, using this one-way function, she still will not be able to work out the value of x, which is the cipher key.

Alice then picks a private number – 2, say – and works out 5^2 (mod 7) is 4 and sends the result to Bob. He also picks a private number – 9, say – and works out 5^9 (mod 7) is 6 and sends this to Alice. It does not matter that Eve is listening, as 2 and 6 are not the key.

To discover the key, Alice takes Bob's number and raises it by her private number, which gives 6^2 (mod 7) = 1. Meanwhile, Bob takes Alice's number and raises it by his private number, 4^9 (mod 7) = 1. Both Alice and Bob end up with the same number, so 1 is the key. They have agreed on a key without meeting up or transmitting it over an insecure line. And Eve cannot work out what the key is because she does not know Alice and Bob's private numbers. Alice does not know Bob's number and Bob

does not know Alice's because they have not been exchanged.

Eve could, of course, run through all the possibilities until she hits on the right one. But DES uses much larger numbers as keys, so this would take a very long time.

The asymmetric cipher

Diffie then came up with a new idea – the asymmetric cipher. Until that point, all ciphers had been symmetric; the same key was used to encrypt and decrypt. Decrypting was simply the reverse of encrypting, hence the cipher was symmetrical. Diffie's idea was to have a cipher where the encryption key and the decryption key were different. The encryption key could then be made public, so that anyone would encipher a message with it. But only someone with the decryption key could read the message – it would be kept private.

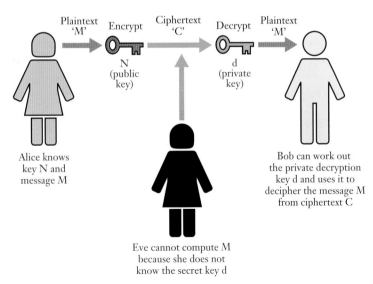

Alice knows key N and message M

Eve cannot compute M because she does not know the secret key d

Bob can work out the private decryption key d and uses it to decipher the message M from ciphertext C

Asymmetric encryption: the plaintext is encrypted using a public key and decrypted using a different private key.

WHITFIELD DIFFIE (1944–)

Interested in codes and ciphers since a child, Whitfield Diffie graduated with a BSc in mathematics from MIT, where he began programming computers. A pacifist, Diffie went to work for MITRE, a defence contractor, to avoid the draft during the Vietnam War. He then moved to the Stanford Artificial Intelligence Laboratory, but quit to pursue his interest in cryptography. Visiting IBM's Thomas J. Watson Research Center, he was advised to contact Martin Hellman, a professor at MIT who was running a cryptographic research programme. Together with Ralph Merkle they developed the idea of a dual-key or public-key cryptography, known as the Diffie–Hellman–Merkle key exchange.

Bansky's 'Spy Booth' on the side of a house in Cheltenham, less than three miles from GCHQ. Although the mural was listed, it was removed in 2016. However, GCHQ have used the image on their website.

Using the padlock analogy again, anyone can lock a padlock simply by clicking it shut. But only someone with the key can open it. Anyone can have one of Alice's padlocks and lock their message in a box with it, but only Alice has the key to open it. The hunt was on for a mathematical function which would work that way.

At MIT's Laboratory for Computer Science, computer scientists Ron Rivest and Adi Shamir and mathematician Leonard Adleman came up with the answer – the RSA cryptosytem. This uses a one-way function as before, but here Alice creates a key by multiplying two large prime numbers, 'p' and 'q', together – p x q = N. These two numbers are her private key and she keeps them to herself. Their product 'N' is part of the public key which she distributes to all and sundry along with a number we shall call 'e'.

In a computer system, text is usually encoded as ASCII or some other form of binary code. So it is already, essentially, a number. We will call the plaintext the number M and we will call the ciphertext the number C. The one-way function we will use is:

$$C = M^e \pmod{N}$$

Bob picks 'p' to be the prime number 17 and 'q' to be 11, and keeps them both secret. But he publishes the public key N, which is 17 x 11 = 187, along with e = 7, say. Let's say Alice's message to Bob is simply her initial, the capital letter A, which is 65 in ASCII. She then encrypts her message:

$$C = 65^7 \pmod{187} = 142$$

To decrypt the message, Bob has to work out his decrypt key, d, using the formula:

$$d = 1 \pmod{(p - 1) \times (q - 1)}/e$$

So:

$$d = 1 \pmod{16 \times 10}/17 = 1 \pmod{160}/7 = 23$$

To decrypt Alice's simple message, Bob uses the formula:

$$M = C^d \pmod{187}$$
$$M = 142^{23} \pmod{187}$$
$$M = 65, \text{ which is A in ASCII}$$

Naturally, in the real world of computer encryption, the values picked for 'p' and 'q' are huge. But they are easy to multiply together to give the public key. However, once you have the public key, factorizing it back into two prime numbers is immensely difficult. The only way to go about it is to take one prime number at a time, divide the public key by it, and see if you get a remainder. If you don't, then the prime number you have picked is 'p' and the quotient is 'q'.

A general view of the 24-hour Operations Room inside GCHQ in Cheltenham, England, in November 2015.

RSA-768

There are regular challenges to factorize huge RSA keys into prime numbers. A recent one to be cracked was RSA-768, which ran to 232 decimal digits or 768 bits. It was:

12301866845301177551304949583849627207728535695953347921973224521517264
005   07263657518745202199786469389956474942774063845925192557326303453 73
15482685079170261221429134616704292143116022212404792747377940806653514
19597459856902143413

It took French computational mathematician Paul Zimmermann and 12 colleagues two years to work out:

p = 33478071698956898786044169848212690817704794983713768568912431388982 88
37938780022876147116525317430877378144467999489
q = 36746043666799590428244633799627952632279158164343087642676032283815 73
96665112792333734171433968102700927987363089 17

Though public-key encryption is not unbreakable, at least theoretically, it is unbreakable in practice until someone comes up with a shortcut in factorization.

Forerunner

Although Diffie, Hellman and Merkle, then Rivest, Shamir and Adleman, were credited with the creation of public-key encryption, it has since been discovered that it was first invented by James Ellis at GCHQ in the 1960s. However, news of his breakthrough was suppressed by the Official Secrets Act.

While Ellis came up with the idea of public-key cryptography he was not a mathematician, and others in GCHQ were tasked with making it a reality. For three years, the brightest minds in the organization tried and failed.

Then a young Cambridge graduate named Clifford Cocks arrived at GCHQ. Unaware of its importance and having nothing else to do, he applied himself to the problem. Later, he recalled: 'From start to finish, it took me no more than half-an-hour. I was quite pleased with myself. I thought, "Ooh, that's nice. I've been given a problem and I've solved it."'

He had come up with what was later known as RSA and people he didn't know were approaching him in the corridors and congratulating him. Fellow GCHQ cryptographer Malcolm Williamson was determined to prove him wrong and, against all regulations, took the problem home with him. He spent five hours on it, but was unable to find a flaw. Instead he came up with another solution to key distribution, which was essentially the Diffie–Hellman–Merkle key exchange.

In the USA, the Diffie–Hellman–Merkle key exchange and RSA became immensely successful commercial products. But the British inventors were sworn to secrecy as GCHQ had no interest in announcing their invention to the world. They wanted to hold on to it to protect British secrets, though in the spirit of transatlantic cooperation they did share the information with the NSA.

Although Ellis never received the recognition he deserved while he was alive, he was sanguine. 'Cryptography is a most unusual science,' he wrote. 'Most professional scientists aim to be the first to publish their work, because it is through dissemination that the work realizes its value. In contrast, the fullest value of cryptography is realized by minimizing the information available to potential adversaries. Revelation of secrets is normally only sanctioned in the interests of historical accuracy after it has been demonstrated that no further benefit can be obtained from continued secrecy.'

In the modern world, public-key encryption makes online financial transactions secure. It is thought that half the world's Gross Domestic Product travels via the Society of Worldwide International Financial Telecommunications (SWIFT) which provides secure communications between banks.

MEETING IN THE PUB

Diffie heard rumours that Ellis had beaten them to the punch, possibly from contacts in the NSA who shared a great deal of secret information with GCHQ. In 1982, he flew to England and met Ellis in a pub in Cheltenham. But every time Diffie approached the topic of cryptography, Ellis changed the subject. Eventually, just before they parted, Diffie asked: 'Tell me how you invented public-key cryptography.'

Ellis said: 'Well, I don't know how much I should say. Let me just say that you people did much more with it than we did.'

FIVE EYES

Following on from the wartime BRUSA Agreement, sharing intelligence, the UK and USA signed the UKUSA Agreement in 1946. Under it, the NSA at Fort Meade and GCHQ in Cheltenham share the signals intelligence they obtain from taping phone cables and intercepting radio transmissions. Canada joined the UKUSA Agreement in 1948, followed by Australia and New Zealand in 1956 – making up the 'Five Eyes'. Other nations were included in an eavesdropping network called Echelon. Norway joined in 1952, Denmark in 1954 and Germany in 1955. Italy, Turkey, the Philippines and Ireland were also members.

Some 6,000 people work in the Doughnut building, GCHQ's headquarters in Cheltenham, Gloucestershire. Along with Fort Meade, Maryland, it is one of the key hubs of 'Five Eyes'.

CHAPTER 16

THE END OF CODEBREAKING AS WE KNOW IT?

'There will come a time when it isn't "They're spying on me through my phone" anymore. Eventually, it will be "My phone is spying on me".'

Philip K. Dick,
science fiction author

With websites, emails, smart phones and hacking, warfare has now gone online. And on the internet everything is encoded and needs decoding. The NSA and GCHQ now trawl huge numbers of innocent calls looking for evidence of wrongdoing. Meanwhile, researchers are investing quantum effects to make communication totally secure.

The job of those trying to keep track of us is made much easier as most people carry mobile phones, whose camera, microphone and GPS facility can all be switched on remotely.

The digital revolution

Codebreaking is now the job of GCHQ, the NSA and other secretive organizations who are not about to tell us what they are up to. They oppose strong encryption because of the dangers of criminals and terrorists using it to go about their nefarious activities. On the other hand, without strong encryption the security services are free to read all our emails and other private transactions online. There are some cryptologists who think we should value our privacy and are prepared to fight back. One such is Philip Zimmermann.

An anti-nuclear weapons campaigner in the 1980s, Zimmermann began to warn of the dangers of the digital revolution and the need for strong encryption. 'Cryptography used to be an obscure science, of little relevance to everyday life,' he said. 'Historically, it always had a special role in military and diplomatic communications. But in the Information Age, cryptography is about political power, and in particular, about the power relationship between a government and its people. It is about the right to privacy, freedom of speech, freedom of political association, freedom of the press, freedom from unreasonable search and seizure, freedom to be left alone.'

He pointed out that, in the past, if the government wanted to violate the privacy of ordinary citizens, it had to go to the trouble of intercepting and steaming open letters, or tapping phones and listening into private conversations. It was labour intensive and could not easily be practised on a large scale. But email messages are all too easy to intercept and scan for keywords on an industrial scale. According to Zimmermann, this made 'a quantitative and qualitative Orwellian difference to the health of democracy'.

It was up to cryptographers to protect the individual against a government that could track every movement of the political opposition, every financial transaction, every communication, every email and every phone call using voice recognition and transcription software.

In 2006, the movie The Lives of Others *depicted the monitoring of the people of East Berlin by the secret police (Stasi) during the Cold War.*

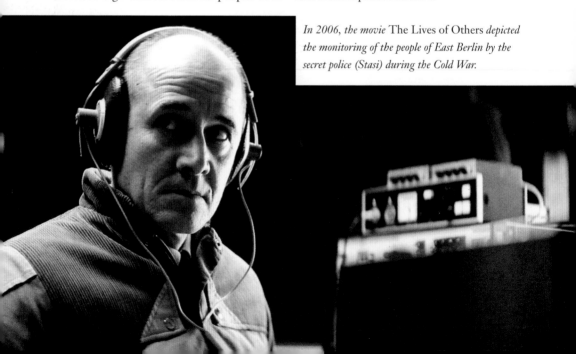

Pretty Good Privacy

Zimmerman saw RSA as a step forwards, as individuals created their own public and private keys. But asymmetric encryption requires a good deal of computing power, so its use favoured the government and large corporations. Zimmermann thought everyone had the right to privacy.

First, he came up with a way to speed up the use of RSA on a personal computer. The message itself would be enciphered using a symmetric-key block cipher called the International Data Encryption Algorithm, or IDEA. Only the IDEA key would be enciphered using RSA. That way it could be passed securely. To do this, he developed a program named PGP – Pretty Good Privacy.

There was still the problem of generating a key. Alice (see page 187) would have to come up with two large prime numbers and multiply them together each time she wanted to send a message. Zimmermann came up with an easy way to do this, which he incorporated in PGP. All Alice had to do was wiggle her mouse. Its random movement would generate a random set of private and public keys.

Electronic signature

Another feature Zimmermann added was an electronic signature. When a message is transmitted using a public key, anyone could have sent it, so the system is open to widespread fraud. A bank might receive a message telling it to withdraw money from an account, but it would have no assurance that the instruction came from the person whose bank account it was.

> 'It's time for cryptography to step out of the shadows of spies and the military and step into the sunshine and embrace the rest of us.'
>
> Philip Zimmermann

Diffie and Hellman had realized that if you separated the public key from the private key, as well as using the public key to encrypt the message and the private key to decrypt it, the process would work the other way around. There was little point in pursuing this as it provided no security at all. What was the point of encrypting a message if the key to decrypt it was publically available, so everyone could read it?

However, Zimmermann realized that if the message was encrypted using the private key it must have come from the person concerned, as he or she was the only one with access to it. Zimmermann incorporated in PGP a two-stage encryption process. First, the message was encrypted using the sender's private key; second, the result was encrypted using the recipient's public key. That way, only the recipient could decrypt it using their private key. Then they would decrypt the result using the sender's public key, confirming that it had really come from them.

PGP and the law

The US government was not happy that a secure system which the NSA could not break was about to be launched. So in 1991, the Senate introduced an anti-crime bill that included a clause, saying: 'It is the sense of Congress that providers of electronic communications services and manufacturers of electronic communications service equipment shall ensure that communications systems permit the government to obtain the plain text contents of voice, data, and other communications when appropriately authorized by law.'

This would have forced manufacturers of secure communications equipment to insert special 'back doors' in their products; a back door is a way round a computer's security system which means that the government can read anyone's encrypted messages. To pre-empt Congress, Zimmermann published PGP as a free software. Ultimately, the clause was dropped from the bill amid howls of protest.

The National Security Agency (NSA) Utah Data Center stands under construction in Bluffdale, Utah, on 4 July 2013.

While human-rights groups praised Zimmermann, he came under fire from RSA Data Security Inc. for infringing its copyright. The authorities then accused him of arms dealing. Under US law, encryption software was classified as a munition and he had exported it by publishing it on the internet.

The investigation of Zimmerman and PGP provoked a debate. While the law-enforcement and security agencies maintained it was necessary to read personal communications to prevent terrorism and crime, civil libertarians insisted that people had the right to privacy. Private citizens needed protection from the authorities' snooping, citing the illegal wiretaps that the government had used in the past.

The communications intelligence agencies themselves are under attack by hackers.

The business lobby is also in favour of strong encryption. Not only does it secure transactions over the internet, it also provides some protection against hackers. But as in the past, the race is on between the codemakers and the codebreakers.

Key escrow

As a compromise, a system of 'key escrow' was proposed. The idea was that the private keys would be lodged securely with a trusted third party and could only be obtained by the authorities if there was sufficient evidence to obtain a warrant. The NSA came up with an algorithm to do this called 'Skipjack', carried on a so-called 'Clipper' chip. The two parts of the private key were lodged with separate institutions: one with the National Institute of Standards and Technology (NIST) and the other with the Automated Systems Division of the US Treasury.

The US government used Clipper for its communications and insisted that all companies involved in government business adopt the US Escrowed Encryption Standard. Outside the government, there was little enthusiasm for Clipper as it was thought there was a danger of the escrowed decryption keys being obtained by unauthorized persons or misused by overzealous government agencies.

Another problem was that as Skipjack had been developed secretly by the NSA it had not been peer reviewed. Soon after it was introduced in 1994, cryptologists began to pick holes in the system and by 1996 it was defunct.

Other means of attack

By the end of the last century, there were around 260 million personal computers in the world. The NSA complained that if they were all put to work on a single message encrypted using PGP it would take 12 million times the age of the universe to break it. But history is littered with so-called unbreakable codes.

Even if the text of a PGP cipher cannot be broken easily, much can be gleaned from traffic analysis: who is sending a message to whom can speak volumes. There is

The whistle-blower Edward Snowden revealed how the NSA and GCHQ trawl through our phone calls, texts and emails, and log every move we make on the internet.

also the so-called tempest attack. Anything electrical – such as a keyboard – gives off radio waves. A detector van parked outside your house is able to pick up a message in plaintext as you are keying it in, before it is encrypted. By using the motion sensor inside a smartphone, a surveillance officer can log the user's keystrokes. It is even possible to infect PGP software with a virus which notes the user's private keys and sends them to the snooper via the internet. Or the machine can be hacked with a Trojan horse, allowing the snooper backdoor access.

The leaking of a large cache of top secret documents by whistleblower Edward Snowden in 2013 showed that the NSA, GCHQ and other intelligence agencies were involved in electronic surveillance on a global scale.

Quantum computing

Cryptanalysts are still looking for a way to break the RSA cipher (see page 188). This depends on factoring. It is a procedure that mathematicians have been studying for centuries, but no one has yet found a shortcut; or, if they have, they're not telling.

One way forward is to use a quantum computer. This uses quantum mechanical effects to do numerous calculations at the same time, rather than handling them one at a time like a conventional processor. Oxford physicist David Deutsch came up with the idea in 1985. Then, in 1994, Peter Shor at AT&T's Bell Laboratories in New Jersey developed an algorithm for integer factorization which would break the public key used in RSA in the blink of an eye. The problem was that Shor's algorithm had to run on a quantum computer.

DAVID DEUTSCH (1953 –)

Born in Israel, David Deutsch was educated in England, where he wrote his PhD thesis on quantum field theory in curved space-time. In 1985, he produced a ground-breaking paper on quantum algorithms that introduced the idea of quantum computing. His 1997 book, *The Fabric of Reality*, outlined his theory of everything for a general audience. In 2008, he became a Fellow of the Royal Society and in 2011 he published *The Beginning of Infinity: Explanations that Transform the World.*

In 2013, a quantum computer made by the Canadian company D-Wave was bought by a consortium including Google and NASA. Then, in August 2016, researchers at the University of Maryland built the first reprogrammable quantum computer. Its process contains just five charged atoms trapped in a line by a magnetic field. While traditional computers can handle only bits – which can be either a 1 or a 0 – a quantum processor uses quantum bits, or qubits, that can be either a 1 or a 0, or both at the same time in a state known as superposition. It has already been shown to solve three algorithms in a single step, something which would require several operations in a normal computer. Once a full-scale quantum computer is up and running, no conventional cipher is secure.

If quantum effects can be used to break codes, they can also be used to make them. In a thought experiment, physicist Stephen Wiesner devised a way to produce an unforgeable banknote. His idea was to have a series of light-traps on the note, which contained photons of light whose polarization corresponded to the serial number of the note. To simplify matters, the polarization would be at 0, 35, 90 and 135 degrees, say, and they would be read by Polaroid filters that were either vertical or at a 45-degree angle.

The bank itself would hold a table of the serial numbers and the polarization of the photons and could simply read them off to prove that the note was genuine.

PETER SHOR (1959–)

After gaining his degree in mathematics from Caltech in 1981, Peter Shor earned his PhD in applied mathematics at MIT in 1985. After a year at the University of California at Berkeley, he moved to Bell Laboratories where he developed Shor's algorithm for integer factorization. It was first demonstrated at IBM using a quantum computer with seven qubits in 2001. Two years later, Shor moved back to MIT, where he became professor of applied mathematics.

The work of a forger who used photons at random would be spotted immediately. To make a counterfeit copy of a note, the forger would have to read the polarization of the photons. If a vertical filter had been used, photons at 0 and 90 degrees would either be passed through or blocked, giving a 1 or a 0. Quantum effects mean that half the photons at 45 and 135 degrees get through but, in the process, the orientation will have been changed to vertical. The forger will not be able to tell if the photon was originally polarized vertically, or polarized diagonally and turned to the vertical by the filter.

STEPHEN WIESNER (1942–)

As a graduate student at Columbia, Stephen Wiesner discovered several important ideas in quantum information theory. Although his fanciful notion of quantum money remained unpublished for over a decade, it was key in the development of quantum key distribution.

Clearly, the technology did not exist to make Wiesner's quantum money and no journal would publish an article on such an abstruse idea. But his friend Charles Bennett talked about it to his friend Gilles Brassard, a computer scientist at the University of Montreal, and they realized it had an application in cryptography.

Imagine two computers connected by fibre-optic cable. A series of polarized photons could be sent down the cable representing 1s and 0s, depending on their orientation. Some would be vertical, some horizontal and some polarized in either

of the two diagonals. As the message is transmitted, the sender moves the Polaroid filter between vertical and diagonal.

The recipient also switches their Polaroid filter around and notes the results. Then the sender tells the recipient what the orientation of the Polaroid filter was for a random sequence of digits. The recipient can now mark off which ones they have got correct. The rest are discarded.

Fibre-optic cable connected to a single patch panel.

What the sender has succeeded in doing by this process is sending a secure key that cannot be read on the way. If the telephone line is tapped, all the eavesdropper can hear is the orientation of the filter in each case, not the value of the digit itself. And if the fibre-optic cable has been tapped, it is easy for the recipient to discern.

Not knowing the polarization of the photons, the third party can only guess and orientate their filter at random. This means that if a diagonally-polarized photon hits a vertical or horizontal filter, its orientation will be altered in half the cases. And if a vertically or horizontally polarized photon hits a diagonal filter, its orientation will also be altered in half the cases. In this case, the sender and recipient would check the line and start again.

When they do manage to send the key without anyone intercepting it, they can use it with a one-time pad, which is truly unbreakable.

Bennett and Brassard (see box above) managed to send a message across the lab using this system. The world's first bank transfer made using quantum key distribution was carried out in Vienna in 2004 and a network using 200km (124 miles) of standard fibre-optic cable was set up there in 2010. There are other quantum networks in Geneva, Tokyo, Massachusetts and around the Los Alamos National Laboratory in New Mexico. While these are believed to be secure, we can only wait to see whether a new generation of codebreakers will find a way to penetrate them. The story of codebreaking suggests there is always a way to do it.

Harnessing modern physics, there seems no limit to what computers can do.

GLOSSARY

ASCII American Standard Code for Information Interchange, a set of digital codes representing letters, numerals and other symbols widely used for the manipulation of text in computers.

Asymmetric-key cryptography A cipher where the key for enciphering is different from the one required for deciphering.

Bigram A group of two letters that may be encoded as a unit.

Caesar-shift substitution cipher Originally a cipher where a letter is replaced by another letter three places further on in the alphabet (A by D, B by E, C by F and so on). More generally, it is a cipher where each letter is replaced by a letter a set number of places further on in the alphabet.

Cipher Where a message in plaintext is encoded letter by letter.

Cipher alphabet The list of letters that are substituted for others.

Ciphertext The message once it has been enciphered.

Cleartext In clear or plain language.

Code Where one codeword or code number is substituted for a word or phrase in the plaintext.

Codebook A list of replacements for words or phrases.

Codetext The message once it has been encoded.

Commercial code A code used by businesses that was originally devised to save on the cost of cables, as telegraph companies frequently charged by the word.

Cryptanalysis The act of deciphering or decoding a message by an unauthorized person who does not know, initially, how it was enciphered or encoded.

Cryptanalyze To break a cipher or code.

Cryptogram An encrypted message ready for transmission.

Cryptography The art and science of enciphering and encoding.

Cryptology The science of cryptography and cryptanalysis.

Decipher To unscramble an enciphered message and render it in plaintext.

Decode To unscramble an encoded message and render it in plaintext.

Decrypt To decode or decipher.

DES Data Encryption Standard.

Diffie–Hellman–Merkle key exchange A method of transferring a secret key without risk of it being used by anyone who intercepts it.

Digital signature A method for confirming the source of an electronic document.

Digraph Another word for a bigram.

Encipher To disguise a plaintext message by substituting each letter with another letter, number or symbol.

Encode To disguise a plaintext message by substituting each word with another from a codebook.

Encrypt To encode or encipher.

GC&CS Government Code and Cypher School.

GCHQ Government Communications Headquarters.

Homophones A number of different letters, numbers or symbols that can be substituted for one letter in the plaintext.

Ideograph or ideogram A written character symbolizing the idea of a thing without indicating the sounds used to say it, as in Arabic numerals and Chinese characters.

Key An arrangement of letters setting a cipher alphabet or the settings of a cipher machine, often existing as a keyword, keyphrase or keynumber for ease of recall, or the element that turns a general encryption algorithm into a specific method of encryption.

Key distribution The process by which the recipient of an encrypted message gets the key to decrypt it.

Key escrow A method by which secret keys come be lodged with a trusted third party so, if necessary, they can be accessed by the authorities.

Key length The number of digits or bits in the key.

Monoalphabetic substitution Where one letter is always substituted for another in the plaintext.

Nomenclator A list of names that can be substituted one for another.

Nulls Letters, numbers or symbols that mean nothing, but are added to confuse anyone intercepting a message and trying to decode it.

One-time pad Encipherment using a random key which is the same length as the message, so each cipher alphabet is used only once. The only known form of encryption that is unbreakable, both in theory and practice.

Plaintext The message before it is encoded.

Polyalphabetic substitution When two or more cipher alphabets are used in a prearranged manner when encrypting a message.

Polygram A group of more than two letters that maybe encrypted as a unit.

Pretty Good Privacy (PGP) A computer program for encrypting and decrypting data that is secure and provides authentication of the source.

Private key A secret key known only to the recipient used to decrypt a message in public-key cryptography.

Public key An openly available key used to encrypt a message in public-key cryptography.

Public-key cryptography An asymmetric cipher used to encrypt a message using an openly available public key and decrypted by a private key only known to the recipient.

Quantum computer A computer which uses quantum effects to perform multiple actions simultaneously.

Quantum cryptography A form of cryptography which depends on quantum effects to transmit the key for a one-time pad securely, making it unbreakable.

Steganography Concealing the existence of the message, using invisible ink, microdots and other methods of hiding it.

Substitution cipher Replacing letters with other letters, numbers or symbols.

Super-encipherment A code that has been enciphered, or a cipher that has been re-enciphered one or more times.

Symmetric-key cryptography The type of cryptography where the key to encrypt and decrypt a message is the same.

Transmission security Sending a long radio message in a single short burst.

Transposition cipher A systematic jumbling of the order of letters in plaintext.

Vigenère cipher A polyalphabetic cipher that uses 26 separate cipher alphabets, each Caesar-shifted by a different number of places.

INDEX

PICTURE CREDITS